CENTRAL ASIA:
IN SEARCH OF A
NEW IDENTITY

Igor P. Lipovsky

ISBN-10: 1-4783-0339-5
EAN-13: 978-1-4783-0339-8
Library of Congress Control Number: 2012913538
CreateSpace, North Charleston, SC

In loving memory of my father
Pavel I. Lipovsky
1914-1994

CONTENTS

Introduction

The unexpectedly rapid disintegration of the USSR has created a completely new political situation in the former Soviet national republics. Whilst almost everywhere the communist leadership has lost its position of power, in Central Asia events have taken a different turn. In all five Central Asian republics the former party elite has not only remained in power, but has managed to maintain a greater degree of political and economic stability than anywhere else in the former USSR (with the exception of Tadjikistan). Notwithstanding this, in Central Asia too there have been serious changes in the balance of political power. The former communists have had to accept the appearance of three new political forces: nationalists, Islamists and democrats. The nationalist opposition is strongest in the three Turkic republics: Kazakhstan, Uzbekistan, Kyrgyzstan. In distinction to the nationalists, the Islamic fundamentalists are a real force only in Farsi-speaking Tadjikistan, and the democrats only in Kazakhstan, where Russians make up a large percentage of the population. It is nevertheless true that the strongest positions in all five republics are still held by the ex-communist leadership. It is no secret that the Central Asian republics were those least affected by Gorbachev's reforms. Whilst even in the central regions of the USSR 'perestroika' and 'glasnost' had a superficial character and did not lead to any serious economic or social progress, in Central Asia - on the very edge of the country - local leaders did not even always consider it necessary to carry through cosmetic, purely external changes. In Central Asia, unlike other Soviet republics, the break-up of the USSR was perceived by the leadership as a negative and dangerous development; the Central Asian leadership provided the only genuine resistance to this break-up. This position can be explained by a number of serious motivations. Firstly, from an economic point of view, the Central Asian republics were unable to function properly without the enormous financial subsidies provided by the centre; these subsidies constituted from one to two thirds of the republics' budgets. Secondly, the republic's economies were bound by a thousand threads to the central economic mechanism; the severing of even some of these threads could have paralyzed the Central Asian economy. According to Soviet economists, at the end of the 1980s there was no such economic region as Central Asia, in as much as the economic links between these republics did not exceed 10% of the republics' links with other regions of the USSR[1]. Each of these republics had significantly wider economic contacts with the centre, i.e. with the Russian Federation, than with its neighbours. This direct link with the centre led to Central Asia having neither a unified economy, nor a single administration, nor even minimal economic coordination. Reorienting the area's economic links would have taken many years and been prohibitively expensive for Central Asia's uncompetitive (even by Soviet standards) industry and backward, unprofitable agriculture. In its present form the Central Asian economy could have functioned normally only in the context of the unified economic zone of the USSR; modernization and structural rebuilding of the economy would have required the investment of enormous sums of money, which could never have been found within Central Asia itself. Even if the entire Central Asian cotton harvest were to be sold on the international market for hard currency, this would not compensate the region's economic losses for the disruption of its links with the centre.

The removal of the CPSU[2] from power and the break up of the USSR also conflicted with the interests of the Central Asian leadership for reasons of a political and ideological character. The absolute sway held by the CPSU over Soviet society and the presentation of Central Asia as a constitutive part of a great power gave the Central Asian leadership both the political legitimacy it needed and an ideological foundation for its policies in the eyes of the local population. The link with the centre constituted an irreplaceable source of strength and a guarantee of limitless economic, military, political and moral support for the local leadership. Marxism-Leninism made it possible to smooth over national and territorial conflicts in Central Asia, and justified the ruthless suppression of all forms of opposition - from Islamic fundamentalism to various movements of a national and democratic character. In Central Asia Marxism-Leninism was a kind of ideological wrapping-paper, a convenient form of political power in the traditional style of the old feudal clans of Khiva, Bukhara and Kokand.

The abortive coup attempt of August 1991, the de-communization which followed the coup attempt, and the subsequent break up of the USSR dealt the Central Asian leadership a severe blow, stripping it of political legitimacy and ideological authority in the eyes of the population. Hopes that President Yeltsin and his followers would, at least to some extent, continue with Gorbachev's policy of preserving a unified centralized state proved unjustified. The prevailing view amongst Yeltsin's team was that the Central Asian republics were too heavy a financial burden for the new Russia. The Yeltsinites also feared linking their fates with conservative and corrupt politicians of the 'period of stagnation'. The democrat-reformers planned to move Russia closer to the West and to accelerate convergence with capitalism; amongst such plans there was no place for the extremely backward Soviet republics of Central Asia. Thus the Central Asian communist leaders were left to the mercy of fate, confronted with a difficult dilemma: either to abandon their positions and share the fate of their bankrupted bosses, or to hang on to power and find new forms of policy and ideology as well as new allies and new sources of finance. Fortunately for the Central Asian communists, the opposition they faced - a motley mixture of nationalists, Islamists and democrats - were as yet too weak to take advantage of the short period of general confusion and paralysis of power which set in after the coup attempt of August 1991. It was a matter of utter simplicity to switch names and symbols: all the Central Asian communist parties changed their names, and Marxist-Leninist symbolism was replaced by traditional and Islamic names and terms. There was no need to make radical changes to the structure of power in the political or economic spheres, since the Soviet totalitarian system fitted perfectly the local traditions of authoritarianism and the extended economic functions of a feudal Asiatic state. The most significant factor contributing to the survival of the ex-communist leadership in Central Asia was the fact that to a significant degree the institutions of a traditional society had remained intact from feudal times. Central Asia, of course, had not undergone the phase of capitalism which breaks down traditional social institutions; and socialism, which had theoretically been called upon to destroy this feudal legacy, was, in the more than 70 years that Soviet rule held sway in the region, unable to fulfil this role. In the version that was built in Central Asia - as in all the republics of the former Soviet East - socialism itself took the form of a model of the feudal type of community. Characteristic of this form of socialism were paternalism, group segregation and the use of a powerful system of compulsion. Soviet researchers themselves used the following terms to describe the power culture and relations within the communist leadership: 'Paternalism, impulsiveness, a willingness to interfere in anything and everything and in relations of all kinds, belief in the infallibility of the patriarch, intolerance of the opinions of others'[3]. The authoritarianism and bureaucracy which regulated Soviet society in its entirety found an organic match in Central Asia's old feudal system with its traditional, hierarchic type of society. It was this circumstance that played a decisive role in making the Central Asian leadership incomparably more viable than its central counterpart.

Chapter One

IN SEARCH OF A NEW POLITICAL IDENTITY

The Turkish Way

Finding a new ideology was a much more difficult problem for Central Asia's former Party elite. Marxism-Leninism had been discredited - at least for the immediate future. No new alternative ideology was forthcoming from the new Russian leadership, which had no clear political programme and no mass political party or organization which could take over the role of the banned Communist Party. Yeltsin himself and the people around him were united not by a common goal, but by a common opponent - the Communist Party and the nationwide structures under its control. In these conditions, the Central Asian leadership, upon their republics so unexpectedly and easily receiving full independence, tried to adapt to Central Asian life the principles of the secular nationalism of Kemal Atatürk. What they found appealing in the Kemalist model were its fundamental principles: nationalism - which they had found lacking in Marxism-Leninism; a secular form of state - a sine qua non for the continuation of their power; etatism - which lay at the basis of the Central Asian economy; and republicanism - which was their guarantee against a return to the absolute forms of rule practised by the Central Asian khanates. In addition, the Kemalist emphasis on national character and revolutionary change gave them unlimited opportunity for the populism and demagogy they had so widely practised in Soviet times. The Kemalist system of political power had been formulated as long ago as the early 1930s; but this basis had been supplemented by the introduction of later innovations such as the principles of the mixed economy and of attraction of foreign capital - principles which had justified themselves not just in Turkey, but also in Third World countries which had likewise sought a way to accelerate convergence with capitalism. From a political point of view, the Central Asian leaders had a natural and complete sympathy for the character of the Kemalist democracy; controlled and directed, as it was, from above, it fitted in beautifully both with the ways of traditional Central Asian society and with the deep-rooted norms of the old Soviet system. The Turkish model also seemed attractive given the fact that Turkey and Central Asia shared very similar social and economic starting-points. For the leaders of Turkic republics another significant factor was Turkey's closeness in ethnic, cultural, linguistic and religious senses. It should not be forgotten that the Kemalist ideology which lies at the foundation of the 'Turkish way' was originally both anti-imperialist and anti-communist in nature, and rejected both exploitation of Islam and any kind of involvement with pan-Turkism. The present leaders of the Central Asian republics are unable to engage in anti-imperialist or anti-communist campaigns. Their flirtations with Islam frequently contradict the consistent Kemalist policy of laicism (secularism). The permanent presence of the Russian Army on Central Asian soil is likewise ill-consistent with the Kemalist principles of national sovereignty. For these reasons the early anti-imperialist version of Kemalism is absolutely unsuitable for the Central Asian leaders, who received independence so unexpectedly and so reluctantly. Late Kemalism, an ideological and political line typified not so much by Kemal Atatürk himself as by his successors, and above all by Ismet Inönü, is a different matter. The marks of late Kemalism were renunciation of anti-imperialism, a course aimed at maximum convergence with the West, encouragement of investment of foreign capital, a gradual withdrawal from the policy of etatism, the introduction of a multi-party system (although one controlled from above), and concessions to Islam combined with retreat from a strictly laicist policy. This explains why, when talking of the attractiveness of the Turkish way, it is this late version of Kemalism that the Central Asian leaders have in mind. In the economic sphere the Central Asian leaders go even further, understanding the Turkish model as implying not merely a mixed economy but also the policy of economic liberalism conducted by Turgut Özal. It has to be admitted, of course, that there can never be any kind of fit between Kemalist ideology and the Marxism-Leninism which prevailed in Central Asia until recently. Not only did Kemal Atatürk not acknowledge the theory of class warfare; he also denied the very existence of the classes in the Marxist sense of the word, whilst being hostile both to communists and to all forms of Marxist ideology and activity. This is the reason why, in replanting the Turkish model on the soil of postcommunist Central Asia, use was made of a well-known conception of the 1920s - that of the Tatar Muslim Marxist Sultan Galiev.

The Sultan Galiev Model

The attraction of this conception was that it combined a number of constructive features taken from three ideological movements with large influence over Central Asia: pan-Islamism, pan-Turkism and Marxism. In Islam Sultan Galiev saw spiritual and ethical ideals which he judged to be important for society. He considered - quite rightly - that Islam, unlike other faiths, is not merely a religion, but an integral system governing the way that people lead their lives - a system, moreover, which can be destroyed only at the risk of provoking a popular explosion of dissatisfaction. As early as the beginning of the 1920s Sultan Galiev proposed a cautious secularization of the Muslim structures in Central Asia, recommending the elimination of extreme and fundamentalist elements, but without destroying the structures themselves, which were in many cases identical to structures of a social nature. What Galiev was proposing was merely the liberalization of these structures - that they should be adapted in line with contemporary life. From this point of view he was the ideological successor of the Jadids, the Central Asian bourgeois reformers and enlighteners of the beginning of the 20th century. From pan-Turkism Sultan-Galiev took the idea of creating a unified state uniting the Turkic peoples: a Turkic republic where the ideals and national aspirations of the Turkic peoples - divided and broken up by the will of history - could be realized. Echoing the hopes of many Central Asian Muslim communists, Sultan Galiev primarily saw in Marxism the eternal striving for social equality and justice. At the same time, though, he was of the opinion that Europocentric Marxism, a product of capitalist industrialist society, did not meet the requirements of Asian life as it was; the Asian peoples needed an alternative communism - a national and Asian version which would suit their level of economic and social development as well as Islamic spiritual values and the

Islamic way of life. It was only much later that Sultan Galiev's ideas were reflected, and to a certain degree actually realized, in the ideology and practice of Arab socialism. The three component elements of this ideology - nationalism (pan-Arabism), Islamism and Marxism - were put to use in differing proportions by the ruling regimes of a number of Arab countries in the 1960s and 1970s. In Egypt, Syria and Iraq the dominant of the three elements was nationalism; in Libya, Islamism; and in South Yemen, Marxism. In all these countries, however, the common denominator was the economic failure of the various forms of national socialism, no matter in what Islamic trappings the latter were decked out or in what proportions they applied this eclectic model. It is worth noting that by the beginning of the 1990s almost all the varieties of national socialism in Asia and Africa alike either had been eliminated by force or had peacefully evolved in the direction of capitalism. The collapse of the socialist system and the break-up of the USSR - the main military ally and provider of moral inspiration for all regimes of a socialist orientation - has removed for a long time to come all desire, both amongst the ruling establishment and amongst the main opposition forces in Asia and Africa, to resort to this model. The ex-communist leadership of the Central Asian states find themselves in a different position. Whilst understanding that the bankruptcy suffered by Marxism-Leninism was both economic and ideological, they nevertheless, in distinction to Yeltsin's entourage, understand well enough that there can be no quick transition from socialism to capitalism: a lengthy transitional period is required, during which time use will have to be made of elements taken from traditional oriental society, as well as from nationalism and Islam. Thus it comes about that the post-communist transitional period has made Sultan Galiev's ideas relevant once more.

In general, the ideological searchings of the ex-communist elite in Central Asia reveal the following basic components:

In economics: an attempt to find a golden mean between the economic liberalism practised by Turgut Özal in the 1980s and the late Kemalist policy on a mixed economy developed during Ismet Inönü's rule in the years 1961 - 1965.

In home affairs: clear preference is given to the type of controlled democracy that was characteristic of the Republican People's Party in 1946 - 1950.

In the social sphere: use is made of the ideas of the Muslim Marxist Sultan Galiev. These ideas are a sort of connecting link between the Turkish way, the communist past and the present reality as found in the countries of the Muslim East.

This eclectic model, constructed on the basis of the experimental 'Turkish way' and of the unrealized aspirations of the Central Asian Muslim communists, has begun to emerge as the main ideological conception of Central Asia's present leaders. This conception permits the leaders to remain faithful to their communist past whilst, without the need for changes to the structure of power or methods of leadership, making a smooth transition to an ideology of moderate secular nationalism and a mixed economy, and at the same time continuing with the populist policy of 'defending the interests of the people'. In this, the ideology represents the best prospect of finding consensus in society during the difficult period of transition, whilst softening criticism from both the nationalist and the Islamic opposition. The ideological scheme has an important role to play in fulfilling a difficult practical goal: to combine the opportunities inherent in Western capitalism with the ideals of social equality and justice; to adapt Western democratic norms to a system of rigorous Party control; to preserve the secular character of the Central Asian states, whilst making use of elements of Islam. The acceptance of the Turkish way as a basic model objectively reduces the possibility of the pan-Turkic ideology gaining widespread support in Central Asia and elsewhere. Kemalist principles decisively reject pan-Turkism, whilst the emergence and development of modern Turkey is founded on Turkish rather than pan-Turkic nationalism. To the relief of their neighbours, the Central Asian leaders have given a clear preference to the tried and proven Kemalist scheme, as opposed to Sultan Galiev's pan-Turkic idea - an idea which, though appropriate in the 1920s, is so no longer.

There is an additional factor which favours the Turkish model in Central Asia, and this is the clear preference of the superpowers (the USA and Russia) for the Central Asian states to develop along Turkish secular lines rather than in the direction of the Islamic fundamentalism of which Iran is an exponent. On the eve of the visit to the USA of the Turkish prime-minister S. Demirel (elected President of Turkey in 1993), a representative of the US State Department emphasized that Turkey could serve as a model for the Muslim republics of the former USSR. 'We undoubtedly prefer,' he said, 'for Turkish influence to prevail over Iranian. This is in our interests'[4]. Spokesmen for the US administration under Bill Clinton and George Bush alike have repeatedly allowed it to be understood that American support for the ex-communist leadership will continue even in the face of human rights violations in the Central Asian republics, since Central Asia's present leaders are clearly committed to a secular line of development. Russia likewise takes no pains to conceal its preference for a Turkish rather than Iranian orientation for the development of the Central Asian republics[5]. This is well understood by Turkey and provides further motivation for Turkey's fight for its sphere of influence in the region.

The keenest supporter of the Turkish way in Central Asia is Islam Karimov, the President of Uzbekistan. The leaders of the other Central Asian states similarly favour the Turkish model of development, but for various reasons are more cautious in their expressions of support. The former President of Turkmenistan, Saparmurat Niyazov, for example, feared a deterioration of relations with neighbouring Iran. Nursultan Nazarbaev, the President of Kazakhstan, and Askar Akaev, the former President of Kyrgyzstan, were forced to take account of the high percentage of Russians amongst the populations of their republics; these Russian elements look suspiciously upon rapid convergence with Turkey. For this reason Nazarbaev chooses to emphasize Turkish economic experience - above all, in 1) stimulating local entrepreneurship, and 2) attracting foreign capital[6]. Wanting to reassure the Russians and understanding the implications of his republic's specific geopolitical situation, he has repeatedly declared that Turkey cannot become Kazakhstan's main foreign political partner[7].

In distinction to the leaders of the region's Turkic republics, those of Farsi-speaking Tadjikistan (first Nabiev, then Rakhmonov) have endeavoured not to show their preference for the Turkish model in public - firstly, out of a desire not to provoke pro-Turkic nationalist feelings amongst the republic's sizeable Uzbek minority, and, secondly, to avoid complicating relations with their kindred nations, Iran and Afghanistan[8]. However, all the Central Asian leaders without exception have allowed it to be understood, to one extent or another, that: 1) they are in favour of enlightened secularized authoritarianism; and 2) they regard only the latter as capable of overseeing the transition of their republics to democracy and market economics. It is worthy of note that even the Central Asian religious establishment has come out decidedly in favour of the Turkish way. In an interview with the Russian newspaper

'Izvestiya', for example, the head of the spiritual council of Central Asian Muslims, Mufti Mukhamed Yusuf Mukhammad-Sedik categorically denied that Uzbekistan could in the future become a fundamentalist Islamic state. The Mufti emphasized that 'We have a natural sympathy for the Turkish way of development, which is characterized by a secular form of power, economic reforms and Islam'[9]. It is possible, however, that Central Asia's movement in this direction will be suddenly interrupted by the rapid development of events in Russia. In distinction to Central Asia, which has already settled upon a model for its development, Russia has as yet had no notable success in its search for new conceptions in ideology and politics. At the same time its unsuccessful experiment in building a 'consumer society' on Western lines places before it an unpleasant dilemma: either to accept the limitations of an ideology based on Russian nationalism, or to make a return to the supernational ideology in one of its Marxist variations, possibly taking into account the experience of the unfortunate past. Neither of these alternatives promises anything good for Central Asia. In the first case, Russian nationalism will not be able to remain indifferent to the position of millions of Russians presently living in the five Central Asian republics. In the second case, Central Asia will find itself again becoming part of a new centralized state along the lines of the USSR. Thus Central Asian progress along the Turkish path will to no small degree depend upon the development of the situation in Russia itself.

The Idea of a Central Asian Federation

The choice of the Turkish model of development and rejection of pan-Turkism does not imply rejection of the search for unity amongst the Turkic peoples - peoples which were at one time very close to each other. At the very start of Soviet rule communists of Turkic descent actively opposed the decision of the central Communist Party organs in 1924 - 1925 regarding division of the Central Asian peoples into national territories. It is interesting that at the Third Muslim and Fifth Regional Party Conferences in January 1920, Central Asian communists - amongst them leaders such as Turar Riskulov - approved a resolution in favour of the formation of a single unified Turkic republic and the renaming of the Communist Party of Turkestan as 'the Communist Party of Turkic Peoples'. The central organs of the VKP(b)[10], however, overturned these decisions and, in February 1920, sent Turkestan Army Commander Mikhail Frunze, and the Chairman of Turkestan's Division of the Russian Communist Party Yan Rudzutak, to Tashkent to purge party and state institutions of 'pan-Turkic elements' and 'bourgeois deviants'[11]. The most effective method of combating pan-Turkic and pan-Islamic tendencies was considered by the centre to be a policy of division into states and intensive stimulation of national consciousness amongst each of the Turkic peoples. The idea that Central Asia should be divided into separate nations was first propounded by Lenin in 1920, when he proposed dividing Turkestan 'into Uzbekiya, Kirghiziya and Turkmeniya'[12]. Notwithstanding the centre's decision to divide Central Asia into national republics, the local communists continued to speak out against the division of the region and put forward the idea of creating a Central Asian Federation, which they considered to be the highest form of national self-determination. However, this idea too was regarded by the centre as dangerous. It was proposed that proponents of the idea should form member states in preparation for a federation, i.e. separate national republics which could subsequently be united into a federation. But, following the establishment of these republics, the idea of a federation was nevertheless dismissed by the centre as not viable.

The division of Central Asia into national states began in 1924 and was completed only in 1936. It led to the creation of five Soviet republics and two autonomous ones, but, far from resolving the region's national and ethnic problems, actually made their future resolution all the more difficult. Until the beginning of the division almost all the local indigenous peoples - with the exception of the Tadjiks and the Pamirian ethnic groups - had belonged to the Turkic linguistic group and, in spite of large differences in physical type (e.g. between the Turkmens and the Kyrgyz, who belonged to the European and Mongolian races respectively), had shared a common linguistic, cultural and religious heritage. Here emphasis has to be laid on the extremely close kinship, in terms of culture, language and religion, between the Turkic peoples, when compared with that between peoples of the Slavonic, German or Romanic groups. To a large extent this is explained by the fact that the unified Turkic linguistic and cultural community underwent division at a later stage in its development, as well as by the fact that the same ethnic groups merged with different Turkic peoples. For example, the at one time very numerous tribes of Kypchak, whose nomadic existence used to cover an enormous territory, were entirely absorbed amongst the Uzbeks, Kazakhs, Kyrgyz, Karakalpaks, Tatars and Bashkirs. All the Central Asian peoples, including both Turkics and Farsi-speaking Tadjiks alike, but with the exception of a few small Pamirian ethnic groups, belong to the Sunni branch of Islam. At the beginning of the 20th century the majority of Central Asian peoples had a comparable level of development and style of life: the Turkmens, Kyrgyz, Kazakhs and part of the Karakalpaks led a mostly nomadic existence. The Tadjiks and Uzbeks were in the main engaged in agriculture and trade. A

very important feature from the point of view of the ethnic character of Central Asia was the national practice of strip holding characteristic of the region. In Turkestan, which had been established
by the Russian authorities on the site of the Kokand Khanate,
Uzbeks, Kazakhs, Kyrgyz, Turkmens, Tadjiks and Karakalpaks lived
together. In the Bukharian Soviet Republic, created by the
Bolsheviks on the site of the Bukhara Emirate, lived Uzbeks,
Tadjiks and Turkmens. The Khorezmian Soviet Republic, set up
on the site of the Khiva Khanate, was populated with Uzbeks,
Turkmens and Karakalpaks. In terms of numbers Uzbeks were the
dominant nationality in the Republics of Turkestan and Khorezm,
whilst in Bukhara there was an almost equal split between Uzbeks
and Tadjiks. About a third of the population of Khorezm was made
up of Turkmens. National strip holding was characteristic of these
territory-states not only during the Soviet period, but also throughout the history of the Kokand, Bukhara and Khiva Khanates. Their
territories were captured by Russian soldiers in 1864 - 1885, and
subsequently, following the establishment of Soviet rule, were
transformed into Soviet republics. At the basis of national strip
holding in Central Asia lay causes of both a historical and a geographical nature. Ancient Central Asia constituted, together with
the regions of Iran and Afghanistan which adjoined it, an area
populated entirely with a homogenous and closely-related
European population speaking languages of Eastern Iranian origin. From a linguistic point of view, the Pamirian Tadjiks can be
considered the remnants of this, the oldest Central Asian population. From the beginning of our era and throughout the medieval
ages Central Asia was systematically subjected to raids from various
Turkic nomad tribes, Mongoloid in descent. Some of these merged
with the local Farsi-speaking peoples; others, preserving their ra-
cial integrity, continued to live as nomads in the Central Asian

region; whilst for a third group, Central Asia was merely a transitional point on the way to Iran and Asia Minor. Some Turkic tribes were completely absorbed amongst the Farsi-speaking European population, contributing to the latter a number of Mongoloid features (as, for example, can be seen in some Tadjiks); others lost their distinctive Mongoloid features whilst retaining the Turkic language (as was the case with the Turkmens and some of the Uzbeks); still others retained not only their language but also the Mongoloid appearance (as happened with the Kyrgyz and Kazakhs). The turning-point in the Turkicization of Central Asia was the invasion of Genghis Khan at the beginning of the 13th century. The Mongols brought from the East numerous Turkic tribes which, in flooding Central Asia, led to the almost total Turkicization of the region. Arriving on the turn of the 16th and 17th centuries, the Uzbeks were the last large Turkic influx in Central Asia. Right up to the beginning of the 20th century the majority of Turkic peoples in Central Asia continued to lead a nomadic or half-nomadic existence; they included, for example, the Turkmens, the Kazakhs, the Kyrgyz, some Uzbeks and Karakalpaks. The remnants of the region's Farsi-speaking population, on the other hand, - the Tadjiks and some of the settled Turkic Uzbeks - engaged in agriculture and crafts. The numerous invasions; the nomadic, mobile character of the Turkic tribes; wars and processes of assimilation - all this was one cause of national strip holding in Central Asia. Another cause, no less important, was the geography of the region - with its oases convenient for irrigational agriculture alternating with steppes and half-desert fit only for cattle-raising, and with mountainous areas where settled and nomadic forms of agriculture could coexist side by side. Thus, for example, on the eve of the division into national states, the Khodzhentskiy uezd (district) of Samarkandskaya Oblast (province) was populated as follows: on the mountain pasture lands lived nomad Kyrgyz; lower down, in the gorges, lived Tadjiks; still lower down, in the river valleys, were Uzbeks; and in the villages (kishlaks) on the plains lived mainly Tadjiks[13]. Even the Central Asian communist press of the time could not but acknowledge the problems involved in dividing the region into national territories. 'In the territory with a dense Uzbek population there are scattered settlements and nomad camps belonging to the Kyrgyz, whilst in the mainly Kyrgyz territory there are settlements populated with Russian settlers and Uzbeks. Almost all the towns are mainly Uzbek or Russian. Such a state of affairs will lead to much argument over the matter of uniting various settlements with the new republics according to criteria of nationality'[14]. The centre's decision to divide into national territories historically-established states such as Bukhara and Khiva had no national and ethnic justification, and no economic justification either. Neither the Turkic peoples nor the Tadjiks felt any attraction to territorial segregation based on criteria of nationality or to the creation of separate states; an absolute majority of the population felt themselves to be either Turks or Muslims, and not Uzbeks, Tadjiks, Kyrgyz or Kazakhs. For example, in a survey carried out by communists in 1926, the peasants in a large number of areas in Eastern Bukhara answered questions about their nationality by naming their kin and tribe and then by invariably declaring: 'Whether we are Uzbeks or Kyrgyz, that we don't know'[15]. Thus for the great mass of the population national self-identification was less important than a person's awareness of his clan, religious or, at the very best, general ethnic (i.e. Turkic) identity. The ethnic, cultural and linguistic unity of the Turkic peoples was the dominant centripetal force and prevailed over any centrifugal tendencies. Nor was there any territorial-administrative justification for dividing Central Asia along national lines, since the region had always had a well-developed system of national strip holding. Moreover, the Khiva Khanate and the Bukhara Emirate were historically-formed territorial and economic structures which it was senseless to break up. These states - Bukhara (ancient Sogd) in the valley of the River Zeravshan, and Khiva (ancient Khorezm) on the lower reaches of the River Amudarya - were groups of oases bound to each other by strong historical, economic and climatic ties in the midst of the desert and semi-desert which prevails in Central Asia. In this respect the opponents of communism were entirely justified in accusing the latter of inflicting upon the peoples of Central Asia an artificial division into Uzbeks, Turkmens and others whilst destroying ancient historically-established states such as Bukhara and Khorezm. Territorial division of Central Asia according to criteria of nationality did not - and, moreover, could not - resolve national and ethnic problems. Even after the division of the region into five republics, each having a predominance of one of the main Central Asian ethnic groups, all the indigenous peoples nevertheless remained divided; now, though, they were divided by the boundaries of the numerous new republics. For example, according to official figures - which are obviously on the low side - 24% of Tadjiks, 16% of Uzbeks, 12% of Kyrgyz and 7% of Turkmens found themselves outside their own republics, and usually in neighbouring Central Asian republics[16]. These figures, which might seem relatively unimpressive from the point of view of the overall sizes of each of the Central Asian peoples, look rather more troubling when viewed in the context of the republics as considered separately. According to later and more accurate statistics, for instance, a quarter of the population of Tadjikistan is made up of Uzbeks, whilst Tadjiks constitute more than a fifth of the population of Uzbekistan[17]. Some areas of Tadjikistan (e.g. Murgab and Dzhirgatal) are almost entirely populated with Kyrgyz. In

Kyrgyzstan itself, the most important economic regions such as Osh, Dzhalalabad and Uzgen are populated mainly with Uzbeks; for economic reasons, these regions were handed over to Kirghiziya, which was part of the RSFSR[18], in 1924. In the Fergana Valley of Uzbekistan live a large number of Kyrgyz. Still more problematic was the situation in the Autonomous Republic of Karakalpakya, which is situated within the territories of Uzbekistan. A third of the republic's population are Karakalpaks, a third are Uzbeks, and the remaining third Kazakhs. Thus the division of Central Asia into national territories was, at the time of its realization, founded on factors of neither an ethnic, nor a cultural and linguistic, economic or religious character, but is rather to be attributed entirely to the political and ideological motives of the Communist Party central organs - and, above all, to fear of pan-Turkism and pan-Islamism, movements which had nothing in common with the Marxist-Leninist ideology or with the imperial ambitions of Stalin. Just as Moscow had planned, the division of Central Asia into five distinct republics considerably accelerated the formation of separate nations, shaping the amorphous, mainly Turkic mass of the Muslim population into distinct and separate peoples each possessing their own national consciousness, language, culture and economic independence from their neighbours. The formation of separate Central Asian republics threw into question the feasibility of any return to the idea of a pan-Turkic or even pan-Muslim state or federation in Central Asia. Modern history knows of no successful attempt to found a major multi-national state on a purely religious basis. Like the break up of Pakistan in 1971, the evolution of pan-Islamism in the 20th century confirms the non-viability of a similar state in Central Asia. This means that Islam should be regarded only as a connecting link - a link which, however, plays an important role both in relations between the Central Asian republics and in their contacts with the rest of the Muslim world. In Central Asia itself the idea of establishing a single, unified Islamic state is supported mainly by Tadjik fundamentalists. It has to be stressed that of all the Central Asian republics the influence of Islam is felt strongest in Tadjikistan; this is to a large extent to be attributed to the traditional striving of the Farsi-speaking Tadjiks to use Islam as a means of promoting their own integration into Turkic-speaking Central Asia. A similar policy is followed by Iran, which, finding itself squeezed between Arabs and Turks, lays great emphasis on fundamental Islamic values and the need for Muslim unity in an attempt to overcome the considerable ethnic, linguistic and cultural differences dividing it from the Arab world on the one hand, and, on the other, from the numerous Turkic peoples which not only surround Iran but make up a significant part of its own population.

Since the idea of a single Islamic state in Central Asia presupposes a theocratic state, in which, of course, there could be no place for the ex-communist leadership, it naturally meets fierce resistance from those holding the reins of power. In spite of the games they are forced to play with Islam, the present leaders of Central Asia quite rightly regard the Muslim fundamentalists as their most dangerous adversaries and make no attempt to conceal their frank hostility to the latter's plans for establishing an Islamic state even within the boundaries of each Central Asian republic. From the point of view of foreign relations, the Muslim fundamentalists will have to bear in mind the inevitability of direct confrontation both with Russia, which retains hold of important positions in Central Asia, and with USA, whose influence in the region is growing all the time. Moreover, the presence of a large Russian population in republics such as Kazakhstan and Kyrgyzstan makes any attempt to establish an Islamic state on their territories even more difficult. Thus, if plans for a union of all the Central Asian countries within a single Islamic state are utterly utopian, the prospects for an Islamic republic along the lines of Iran in one of the Central Asian republics are weak. Only in one of the five Central Asian republics - Tadjikistan - are the Islamists strong enough to make a claim for power; even here, however, they have little chance of holding on to that power for any length of time. The greatest danger for Tadjikistan, though, is the possibility of a repeat not of the Iranian, but of the Afghan scenario - a bloody civil war between rival political clans.

The idea of establishing a pan-Turkic state is no more realistic. The profound changes which took place in Central Asia during the 74 years of Soviet rule largely destroyed pan-Turkic consciousness, making impossible the realization of the conception of Turkic unity which was once so popular. Pan-Turkism now has as little chance of being realized in Central Asia as has, for example, pan-Slavism or pan-Germanism in Europe, or pan-Arabism in the Near East or North Africa. From this point of view, it would be a mistake to be influenced by the euphoria which gripped Turkish politicians and some Central Asian nationalists after the first free contacts between the two groups following the break up of the USSR. These illusions were expressed best of all at the time by the chief advisor to S. Demirel: 'After our visit to Tatarstan - which is what I call Central Asia - I am firmly convinced of our closeness to the goal which we have dreamt of for so long - the creation of a united Turkish commonwealth'[19]. On the other hand, if 'Turkish commonwealth' means something like the British Commonwealth or even the League of Arab States, then such an arrangement is indeed possible - although no more than possible. It hardly needs to be said that such a 'commonwealth' would be looked on with suspicion by not just Russia, but Iran and China as well, whilst

Tadjikistan would find itself forced into closer relations with the Farsi-speaking world, i.e. with Iran and Afghanistan. In the projected commonwealth the leading role, of course, would be played by Turkey as the strongest and most influential Turkic country. That, however, will inevitably harm Turkey's relations with Russia and Iran, whilst laying an impossible financial burden in terms of support to the Central Asian republics (which are in need of billions of dollars) on the already over-stretched Turkish budget. Given the economic weakness of Turkey, it has to be doubted whether, as things stand and even with the support of the West, she will be prepared to pay such a high price for leadership in a region several thousand kilometres from her frontiers. The most likely prospect of a Central Asian commonwealth might be a partnership between all the Central Asian republics (i.e. not just the Turkic republics) based on bilateral or multilateral agreements, or else an alliance of a consultative character.

On the other hand, the divided nature of the Central Asian peoples, the artificial nature of the boundaries set between them, the fact of sizeable national minorities within each republic - all this could turn into a delayed-reaction bomb threatening to blow apart the political equilibrium both within the Central Asian states and in the relations between them. Serious warning of a future sharp deterioration in all national problems was given by the anti-Russian excesses in Uzbekistan in 1988 - 1989, and subsequently by the pogroms against the Meskhetian Turks and the clashes between Uzbeks and Kyrgyz in the Fergana Valley over shortages of water and land. Even before the break up of the USSR the Central Asian leaders, with the active intermediation of Moscow, tried to smooth over the discontent of a sizeable mass of Tadjiks living in the regions of Bukhara and Samarkand (parts of Uzbekistan); they also tried to solve the problems of the Uzbek population of Tadjikistan. Now that these republics have declared their independence, the friction between Uzbeks and Tadjiks finding themselves in 'the wrong state', has only grown. In Tadjikistan itself a solution is yet to be found for the problem of the so-called Pamirian Tadjiks (an entire group of small peoples speaking eastern Iranian languages as opposed to Tadjik - which is a western Iranian language - and divided by the Pamir mountains from the rest of Tadjikistan). The Tadjik authorities have declared these peoples - who, from a linguistic point of view, are direct descendants of Central Asia's aboriginal population - to be Tadjiks; this takes little account of the specifics of these peoples' language, culture and religion (some are Shiites and even Ismailites). There are also problems in relations between Uzbeks and Turkmens. At a state level these problems were reflected in the conflict over the use of the river Amudarya.

All these interethnic clashes inevitably fuel discussion of the idea of a 'Central Asian Federation'. However, the present-day reality in Central Asia excludes the creation of anything grander than a weak union of a consultative character between the Central Asian states. Unification is possible only 'from above', by means of force, and then only in the event of the restoration of a single centralized state along the lines of the former USSR. It is a fact, however, that in the closing period of its existence, even Soviet totalitarianism had difficulty in finding solutions to the interethnic problems in Central Asia which it had itself given rise to.

Foreign Policy Dilemmas

The ex-communist leadership's search for a new ideological model is made more difficult by the need to develop a new foreign policy without loss of time - and, moreover, in conditions where the independent development of Central Asia is threatened by its highly unfavourable geopolitical situation. Amongst the key factors which have influence over the determination of the Central Asian republics' foreign policy orientation, the following deserve to be emphasized:

1. All Central Asia's neighbours, especially Russia and China, are historically-established states with a large superiority over Central Asia in terms of both military and economic might; in the past they have frequently laid claim to all or part of the territory of Central Asia. With the exception of short periods, throughout the course of its history Central Asia has usually been not a policy-maker itself, but the object of the regional policies of its stronger neighbours. Central Asia has remained independent only when its mighty neighbours have grown weak (which is the case today), and when its territory has been used as a buffer between the rival powers (as happened, for instance, during the Anglo-Russian confrontations in the second half of the 19th century).

2. Central Asia's boundaries with all the states that surround it are of an artificial nature, having been determined not by the interests of the Central Asian peoples but by the military and strategic considerations of the superpowers. As a result of the four Anglo-Russian agreements concluded between 1870 and 1890, for instance, the border between Central Asia, which was an adjunct of Russia, and Afghanistan, which was under a British protectorate, divided a large number of Central Asian peoples (although the division affected these peoples to different degrees). Half of the Tadjik people - including more than half of the Pamirian Tadjiks, - 10% of the Uzbeks and 9% of the Turkmens ended up in Afghanistan. Similarly, the fixing of the border between Russia and Iran

27

left 20% of Turkmens in Iran. The Russo-Chinese border agreement of 1879 left in China 11% of all Kazakhs and 5% of the Kyrgyz. Thus the 'divided peoples' factor threw into question not merely the inviolability of the borders themselves, but also the whole future character of relations between the Central Asian republics and their neighbours. The strengthening of national consciousness amongst the Central Asian peoples following the break up of the Soviet Union also had a noticeable influence on the situation in Afghanistan, where conditions of chronic civil war had given rise to the threat of the country being broken up into its main ethnic groups: Pushtuns, Tadjiks, and Uzbeks.

3. In Central Asia echoes continue to be heard of the former rivalry between two ethno-cultural worlds - Turan and Iran, - i.e. between the Turkic-speaking and Farsi-speaking peoples. Although in Central Asia this ancient conflict finished long ago with victory for Turan, friction between the two sides has not ended, having now crossed over into the sphere of ideology and foreign policy. The Farsi-speaking world, represented by Iran, Afghanistan and Tadjikistan, continues its latent conflict with the expansion of Turkic Turan, as embodied by Turkey and the Central Asian republics of Uzbekistan, Kazakhstan, Kyrgyzstan and Turkmenistan.

4. Following the end of the cold war and the disintegration of the Soviet Union, Central Asia has lost its strategic importance for the West, and is now of interest only from the point of view of resistance to the propagation of militant Muslim fundamentalism. Thus the real rivalry for influence in Central Asia is between its immediate neighbours - Russia, China, Iran and Turkey; the latter, in spite of its physical

distance from the region, considers itself the 'elder brother' of Turkic Central Asia. Another neighbour, Afghanistan, has never been regarded as a serious participant in the struggle for the region, in view of its weakness and traditional policy of non-alignment. Like Central Asia itself, Afghanistan has always been merely an object of competition between the major powers.

In analyzing the prospects of each competitor for Central Asia, attention should be drawn to the following:

Afghanistan. In spite of the fact that it has a common border with three republics (Tadjikistan, Uzbekistan and Turkmenistan), Afghanistan has a real - and, moreover, destabilizing - influence only on the southern part of Tadjikistan.

Iran. In its fight for influence Iran has four trump cards: a) Islam; b) petro-dollars; c) a common ethnic, cultural and linguistic heritage with Farsi-speaking Tadjikistan; d) an extensive shared border with Turkmenistan. Serious minuses for Iran are the following: a) the Shiite character of Islam, ill-suited to the Central Asian Sunnites; b) its openly fundamentalist character, which is unacceptable to Central Asia's ex-communist leadership, nationalists and Muslim establishment; c) its policy of confrontation with the West, to whom Central Asia continues to appeal for aid and assistance.

Iran's influence is felt most strongly in Tadjikistan - firstly because the local Islamists are in a stronger position here than anywhere else in Central Asia, and secondly as a result of the ethnic, cultural and linguistic closeness of the two states. Iran's second main client is Turkmenistan, which, because of the extensive common border it shares with Iran, finds itself obliged to maintain good relations with its dangerous and stronger neighbour. In the remaining three Turkic republics Iranian influence is significantly

weaker than that of its competitors. The leaders of the Turkic republics of Central Asia have repeatedly declared in public that
they find the Iranian way unacceptable[20]

Turkey. Amongst Turkey's clear advantages over its rivals the
following should be emphasized: a) its linguistic and cultural
kinship with Turkic Central Asia; b) the fact of historical and ideological links between the Central Asian Turks and the Ottoman
Empire - e.g. between the Jadids and the Youngturks; c) the attractiveness of the Turkish model of economic development, and
secularization. Highly characteristic in this respect was the announcement by Islam Karimov, President of Uzbekistan: 'I say
unambiguously that the Turkish path of development is more
acceptable to us, firstly as a secular civilized path of societal development. We must work out our own path of development. The
Iranian model is not acceptable to us ... it seems to me that this
is the opinion of Central Asia as a whole'[21]. There is no little
importance in the fact that Turkey is a member of Western alli-
ances and blocs and consequently is able to act as a mediator in
Central Asia's economic and political contacts with the West. At
the same time Turkey suffers from a serious minus in comparison
with its rivals: it is situated a great distance from Central Asia,
which rules it out as an effective military ally - a circumstance is of
no little importance given the unstable and indeterminate situation that presently exists in and around Central Asia. Moreover,
whereas Iran has at its disposal petrodollars, Turkey has more
limited financial means with which to provide the economic aid
so badly needed by the Central Asian states. Nor is the Turkic
card an advantage to Turkey everywhere in Central Asia. In Farsi-
speaking Tadjikistan it gets an altogether negative response; and
in Kazakhstan, where the Russian-speaking population is in the
majority, its use is also highly problematic.

China. Unlike Iran and Turkey, China cannot call upon ethnic, cultural, linguistic or religious closeness to Central Asia. Nor can it use petrodollars to strengthen its influence in the region. However, China is the area's second military power - after Russia - and has in the past frequently laid claim to a part of Central Asia. In consideration of Russia's absorption in internal disorders resulting from the break up of the Soviet Union, and of the Russian leadership's extreme reluctance to use military force outside its own borders, the Chinese factor has unexpectedly gained in importance. Three Central Asian republics find themselves having to pay particular attention to relations with China; they are: Kazakhstan, Kyrgyzstan and Tadjikistan, all of which have extensive common borders with China. For Kazakhstan and Kyrgyzstan these relations are complicated still further by the fact of a sizeable Kazakh and Kyrgyz population in Xingjang, which now belongs to China. From the historical, ethnic and linguistic points of view the province of Xingjang, which is populated with Turkic peoples, has always been closely linked to Central Asia - to such an extent that many historians have considered it more correct to call Xingjang 'Eastern Turkestan' and Central Asia 'Western Turkestan'[22]. Eastern Turkestan became part of the Quing Empire (China) only in the second half of the 18th century, at which time it was given the name 'Xingjang' - meaning 'new frontier' or 'new territory'. According to statistics available for 1953, i.e. before the widespread settlement of Chinese in Eastern Turkestan, 94% of the province's population was made up of Uygurs, Kazakhs and Kyrgyz; moreover, in ethnographic and cultural character, these natives differed little from the Turkic peoples of Central Asia[23]. The declaration of independence by Kazakhstan and Kyrgyzstan was met with concern in China, since independence for the above-mentioned republics has increased self-awareness both amongst the Kazakhs and Kyrgyz of Xingjang, and amongst the Uygurs (95% of whom live in China, and 5% in Central Asia), who are the province's largest Turkic people. The dissatisfaction of the Turkic peoples at the settlement of Chinese in Xingjang, coupled with the growing tendency of the Uygurs for self-determination, and of the Kazakhs and Kyrgyz for reunion with Kazakhstan and Kyrgyzstan, inevitably leads to a deterioration in the relations of these republics with China and compels them to seek help from their traditional patron, Russia.

Russia. Russia continues to hold the most important positions in all spheres of life in the Central Asian republics, being far ahead of its rivals in the struggle for influence in the region. Russia's most important advantage is the fact that Central Asia was part of Russia for more than 100 years and received its independence during the course of internal changes in Russia itself, and not as the result of a protracted struggle. Independence was granted Central Asia unexpectedly and, most importantly, against the wishes of the local Central Asian leadership. The Central Asian republics remain the most obedient member-states in the Commonwealth of Independent States. In Kazakhstan and Kyrgyzstan the large Russian and Russian-speaking population rules out the possibility of those two republics having an independent state policy that does not coincide with the interests of Russia. Until now the ex-communist leaders of Central Asia have been unable to find an alternative patron and donor to take the place of Russia. Neither Turkey nor Iran were able to take on Russia's previous role in the region. It is highly probable that in the event of Russia emerging from its crisis and returning to an active role in the region, centripetal tendencies will again gain the upper hand and the Central Asian republics will take up their places in a new alliance led by Russia. However, the protracted ideological crisis in Russia is paralyzing its Central Asian policy and creating a dangerous political vacuum there. Moreover, the new Russia suffers from the lack of a clear and well thought-out policy regarding Central Asia.

In the final analysis, the foreign policy orientation of the Central Asian states will depend not on factors to do with ethnic, linguistic or religious closeness to, for example, Turkey or Iran, but on the economic and military might of Central Asia's neighbours, and on the extent of their financial assistance available to the new states. In any case, the Central Asian republics will, for a long time to come, remain not so much makers of international policy in the region as the object of their neighbours' policies, especially those of Russia.

Chapter Two

THE RUSSIAN PROBLEM

The annexation of Central Asia to Russia was an exceedingly lengthy and gradual process involving a combination of peaceful and military means. The first people to take Russian citizenship were the Kazakhs, who occupied almost the entire northern half of Central Asia. Squeezed between Jungariya in the East and the Kalmyk Khanate in the West, the Kazakh khans of the Minor and Middle Zhuzes in 1731 - 1743 joined Russia of their own free will in exchange for military support and protection. Considerably later, in the first half of the 19th century, the Senior Zhuz of the Kazakhs also joined the Russian Empire, desiring liberation from the yoke of the Jungars. Kazakhstan, then, transferred to Russian power comparatively peacefully and gradually. In contrast, the southern part of Central Asia had to be annexed mainly by military force. The Russian conquest of the feudal khanates of Central Asia - Khiva, Kokand, Bukhara - occurred comparatively late and lasted twenty years - from 1864 to 1885. The explanation for this lay in the extreme caution of the Russian government, which both feared entering into conflict with England, its constant rival in the East, and was anxious to avoid the financial outlay likely to be incurred in military operations conducted over such a vast territory. Russia had two main uses for its new acquisitions in the East: as a source of raw materials - above all, of cotton; and as a military and strategic bridgehead in Central Asia, giving access to the British possessions in Asia and defending Russian territories around the Caspian Sea, in Southern Siberia and Northern Kazakhstan. There were no plans to colonize these territories by putting in Russian settlers. Moreover, until the end of the 19th century the Russian authorities followed a policy of extreme caution, endeavouring not to infringe upon the economic and religious freedoms of the local Muslim population. The European contingent in Central Asia was at that time of no great size, and consisted mainly of military personnel, Russian civil servants and their families, and a few entrepreneurs and merchants. The Bukhara Emirate and the Khiva Khanate continued to exist as independent states under the protectorate of Russia, thus reducing to a minimum the Russian presence on their soil and giving the Russian administration a limited freedom only on the territory of the former Kokand Khanate, which became the general-gubernatorstvo of Turkestan.

Stages of Russification

The situation began to change in the 1890s. The Russian government was doing everything it could to encourage the cotton-producing business, and at the same time intensive work was carried out on the construction of railways in pursuance of strategic military aims; these were the causes behind the arrival of the first waves of Russian settlers from the central regions of Russia. As a rule, the qualified workers and engineers working in railway construction and in the cotton-producing business were Russians. The first towns in Central Asia to have a purely Russian population also sprang up in places where there were railway stations. The crop failure and famine which struck the central provinces of Russia in 1891 - 1892 aggravated the problems of the Russian peasantry, which had either no land or very little land of its own (in 1861, as is well-known, peasants were given personal freedom from their masters, but no land). In an attempt to control the wave of social tension affecting the centre of the country, the Russian government switched to a policy of encouraging peasant migration to the new lands of the Urals, Siberia and Kazakhstan and Kyrgyzstan. Tajikistan, Uzbekistan and Turkmenistan were not suitable for intensive settlement since they lacked unoccupied land. And so the main target for Russian colonization in Central Asia became the sparsely-populated steppes of Kazakhstan and Kyrgyzia, regions where there was no shortage of vacant land suitable for cultivation. The first wave of Russian settlers was small, and had little real impact on the size of the Russian population in Central Asia. According to the 1897 census, Russians constituted not more than 3% of the overall population of the area now occupied by Uzbekistan, Tajikistan and Turkmenistan, and 10% of areas now forming part of Kazakhstan and Kyrgyzstan[24]. In the same year the Russian government temporarily closed Turkestan to Russian emigration, fearing that the process of colonization there might lead to a lack of pasture-land for the nomads and, consequently, to feelings of discontent amongst the native population. New and larger groups of Russian immigrants appeared in Kazakhstan and Kyrgyzstan after the suppression of the first Russian revolution in 1905-1907. At that time the Russian government, under the leadership of Stolypin, turned to a policy of breaking up the peasant community in the countryside and started actively to encourage the migration of peasants with little or no land from central Russia to the East, where there was a considerable stock of unoccupied land. From this time forwards the Russian government began to take less and less account of the interests of the local nomad population of Kazakhstan and Kyrgyzstan; land was allotted for settlement by Russians at the expense of nomad pasture-land. According to official figures, by 1916 more than 1.3 million peasants had settled in Kazakhstan and Kyrgyzstan i.e. a quarter of the total number of Russians who had emigrated from Central Russia and the left bank of the Ukraine. The speed at which migration occurred was higher only in Siberia and the Far East, areas which attracted 49% of all migrants[25]. In 1917 the Russian share of the populations of Kazakhstan and Kyrgyzstan had grown to 20%, and the percentage of Ukrainians in these territories to 10%[26]; these figures are evidence of the high speed of Russian and Ukrainian immigration into Kazakhstan and Kyrgyzstan at the beginning of the 20th century. Russia's resettlement policy in Central Asia was so intensive that it caused concern amongst the Russian colonial administration. The views of this group of Russian officials were expressed in the reply of K.K. Palen, the Russian senator who conducted an inquiry into the Turkestan general-gubernatorstvo 1908 - 1909. Palen's opinion was that Turkestan should not be used 'as a repository for the surplus population of the land-starved provinces of the centre' - since this policy was obnoxious to 'the indigenous population, who considered themselves injured by the forcible taking away of land and water'. The Russian senator proposed an alternative path for colonization of Turkmenistan: 'a path which would be slower, but fair - to attract the cooperation of Russian business, buy up whatever land is needed and take steps to ensure the supremacy of Russian industry and trade'[27]. This plan, however, was made implausible by the weakness of Russian capitalism, which held control of the markets of the East only thanks to military might.

The consequences of the increase in the size of the Russian population, as well as of the Russian government's departure from its cautious policy of respect for the interests of the natives, became only too apparent during the First World War, when the Tsarist government tried to lay part of the burdens of war on the local population. The imposition of new taxes; the fixing of compulsory low cotton prices; and, finally, the decision to mobilize 250 000 natives for work in the front-line area led to the major anti-Russian uprising of 1916. In many places the rebels put the Russian population to the slaughter, and the local aristocracy and Muslim priesthood announced the formation of an independent khanate, declaring Jihad on Russia. The revolt spread to parts of Turkestan (Bukhara and Khiva, however, took no part), but was quickly suppressed by the Tsar's soldiers; for slaughtering the Russian population, the rebels had their lands confiscated.

The February and then the October Revolutions of 1917 and the Russian civil war of 1918 - 1921 put a halt to the process of Russification in Central Asia and helped to strengthen local national movements, at the same time as contributing to the region's isolation from the rest of the country. The victory of the Bolsheviks in the civil war, however, together with the forcible imposition of the Soviet regime first in Turkestan, then in Bukhara and Khiva, led to the region becoming again firmly attached to Russia. The process of Russification was resumed, although this time it took a different character and form. Instead of Russian peasants migrating to Central Asia, there was an invasion of party functionaries and officials - as a rule, of Russian nationality - sent by the Communist Party to supervise the transition of the tradition-bound local society from feudalism to communism, bypassing capitalism. Unlike Karl Marx, who considered the capitalist stage of development inevitable for the feudal and semi-feudal countries of the East, Lenin was of the opinion that it was possible to make the transition straight to socialism, but only provided that there was supervision and active support from the proletariat of more progressive nations i.e. of Russia. It is interesting to note that according to figures for 1924, 90% of all workers in Party and state organizations in Central Asia were Russian[28]. For fairness' sake, it has to be said that initially the Soviet regime acted in the interests of the local population: in the course of the first stage of the agrarian reforms of 1921 - 1922 lands confiscated from the local peasantry and nomads following the suppression of the revolt of 1916 were returned to their owners; part of the lands earlier given to Russian settlers were also returned. In the shortest possible time steps were taken to put an end to the widespread illiteracy of the local population, women received equal rights with men, steps were taken to improve standards of living and public health.

At the same time, however, the sovietization of Central Asia led not only to the confiscation and collectivization of all forms of property, but also to the annulment of what few political liberties there had been under the rule of the Russian monarchy, and to a forcible and morbid secularization; all of this only helped to accelerate the Russification of the whole region.

The second stage in the Russification of Central Asia was the industrialization which began at the end of the 20s. Lenin's plan for building socialism - the plan which became the programme of the Communist Party - emphasized industrialization as the sine qua non for the development of the new society. It has to be said that industrialization was only made possible in the region due to vast financial subsidies from the centre (these subsidies made up as much as 90% of the total budgetary income of the Central Asian republics). The reverse side of the coin was the arrival in these republics of a large contingent of qualified workers, technical staff and engineers, the great majority of whom were Russian or Russian-speaking. In contrast to pre-Revolutionary times, when the Russian settlers had been drawn from the peasant class and had settled in rural areas, in the Soviet period the immigrants were qualified workers, party functionaries, scientists and people of the artistic world, and settled entirely in the towns.

The third and most important stage in the Russification of Central Asia was the years of the Second World War (1941 - 1945), when vast numbers of people and whole sections of industry were evacuated to the deep rear from districts threatened with German occupation - to the Urals and to Central Asia. For the first time since Central Asia had first been occupied by Russia, the influx of millions of people and hundreds of factories wrought essential changes in the demographic, economic and cultural profile of the whole region. In the course of the war more than 250 major factories - mainly plant-producing in nature - were evacuated to Central Asia; this in turn required prompt expansion of the local fuel and energy system[29]. In the years 1941 - 1945 the Soviet government poured into the economy of Central Asia twice as much money as during the 12 pre-war years of forced industrialization[30].

When the Second World War ended, most of the evacuated factories and the majority of the Russian and Russian-speaking population remained in Central Asia.

The fourth and last influx of Russians into Central Asia was a response to changes in the economic policy of the Soviet Union in the second half of the 1950s. Trying to cover shortages in food production, the central organs of the Communist Party, on the initiative of Nikita Khruschev, approved a far-reaching plan: to plough up and put into cultivation tens of millions of hectares of virgin soil in Kazakhstan (an idea which had previously been considered either inviable or actually dangerous in its possible consequences). Kazakhstan, however, lacked the personnel, agricultural equipment and finance needed for the organization of hundreds of new kolkhozes and sovkhozes. And so in the second half of the 1950s the vast steppes of Kazakhstan saw the arrival of hundreds of thousands of new settlers - mainly from Central Russia - accompanied by large amounts of equipment. This development, which, as time would show, was of highly dubious value from an economic point of view, led to changes in the demographic situation of Kazakhstan. From this time forwards the Kazakhs became the minority not merely in towns and industrial centres, but also throughout most of the country areas of the Kazakh Republic..

On the eve of the disintegration of the Soviet Union the Russian population in Central Asia numbered about 11 million, of whom 8 million lived in Kazakhstan and about 3 million in the other four Central Asian republics. Of the Russians in Central Asia 90% live in towns or cities - 60% of the Russian population in Uzbekistan, for example, is concentrated in Tashkent alone. Until the end of the 1980s, Russians formed the majority in almost all the capitals of Central Asia. Objectively close to the Russians in interests and position is the group of immigrant peoples of various ethnic provenance which appeared in Central Asia during the years of intensive Russification and which is known as 'the Russian-speaking population' in view of the fact that its members adopted the Russian language and Russian culture. Amongst the latter special mention should be made of the Germans forcibly settled in Central Asia by order of Stalin during the Second World War. Before the emigration of Germans to Germany there were about one million Germans living in Central Asia (mainly in Kazakhstan), and they played an important role in the region's economy. Of similar size was the Tatar population , the majority of whom had been exiled, with just as little justice, from the Crimea to Uzbekistan during the Second World War. Similar compulsion was used in deporting 300 000 Koreans from the Far East to the sands and steppes of Uzbekistan and Kazakhstan. The Koreans were the first nationality to suffer repression in the Soviet Union. During 1945 - 1956 Korean settlers in the region were given special passports bearing a stamp forbidding departure, similar to those given to criminals. Nowadays Koreans living in the former Soviet Union have been fully assimilated; very few still speak their native language. Of the Russian-speaking population which moved to Central Asia of its own free will, mention should be made of those with close ties to Russia - the Ukrainians (1 200 000), and the European Jews (120 000), who did not mix with the small local community of Bukharian Jews. The majority of these Russian-speaking peoples suffered greatly under Soviet rule, losing their motherland and native culture and tongue when they were exiled to Central Asia. It is not surprising, then, that in the period during and after the disintegration of the Soviet Union their numbers began to decline sharply. This was a result of, first, the emigration of Germans to Germany and of Jews to Israel; then, of the return of Crimean Tatars to the Crimea and of the migration of Koreans to Central Russia. There has even been talk of repatriating Koreans to Southern Korea. As for the future of those of the Russian-speaking peoples remaining in Central Asia, that is directly linked with the fate of the Russians themselves in that region.

Native Birth-Rate Against Immigration

The stages of the Russification of Central Asia are closely connected with economic, political and ideological changes in Russia itself; moreover, Russification reached its peak in the 40s and 50s of the 20th century, as we know from the statistical evidence. In 1939 - 1959, for example, the percentage of Uzbeks amongst the population of Uzbekistan fell from 64% to 62%, in spite of the fact that the native population increased in size more than one and a half times[31]. A similar situation obtained in other Central Asian republics. From the 60s onwards, however, the situation began to change: the dominant factor in population growth became not Russian migration, but the high birth-rate amongst the indigenous peoples of Central Asia. The table below gives an idea of the growing proportion of natives amongst the populations of the Central Asian republics:

	1959	1970	1979	1989
Uzbeks	62	65	69	74
Tajiks	53	56	59	64
Turkmens	61	64	68	73
Kyrgyz	41	44	48	52

Source: Naselenie Sredney Asii, Moscow, 1985, p.16
Itogy Vsesoyuznoy perepisi naseleniya 1989, Moscow, 1990

In spite of the fact that the number of Russians in Central Asian republics continued to increase until the end of the 1970s, the percentage which they formed of the overall population diminished. Similar developments were to be observed not only amongst the Russians, but also amongst other Russian-language immigrant peoples in Central Asia. In the period 1959 - 1970, for example, in spite of an increase in terms of number, the percentage of Russians amongst the overall population of Central Asia (not including Kazakhstan) fell from 16.3% to 15.1%; at the same time the percentage of Ukrainians fell from 2% to 1.5%, and the percentage of Tatars from 4.2% to 3.7%[32]. In this way by the 1960s differences in the natural growth rate of different populations started to exert a larger influence on ethnic make-up than processes of migration. At the same time, however, it should be noted that in the 1960s and 1970s the birth-rate of the indigenous Central Asian peoples outstripped increases in the Russian population due to natural growth and immigration only slowly; its acceleration became noticeable only in the 1980s and early 1990s. Between the censuses of 1959 and 1970 the native Uzbek population increased in size by 53%, whilst the percentage the Uzbeks formed of the overall population of Uzbekistan increased only by 3% - in spite of the large difference in the natural growths of the Russian and Uzbek populations. This is typical of what happened in other Central Asian republics. That does not, however, mean that we should exaggerate the role of Russian immigration: a considerable factor in determining the general picture in each republic was the presence of other local ethnic minorities with a high birth-rate. A considerable proportion of Uzbekistan's population, for example, is made up of Tajiks; the Uzbeks form a quarter of the population of Tajikistan and 1/6th of the population of Kyrgyzstan. All these peoples, forcibly divided by the borders laid down by the Soviets, share more or less the same level of natural growth; for this reason all changes in the proportion which these peoples form of the overall populations of these republics are to be attributed to growth or decline in the number of Russians and Russian-speaking settlers.

If in absolute terms the Russian and Russian-speaking populations of the Central Asian regions were still growing until the end of the 1970s - whilst the proportion they made up of the overall population was falling, - in the 80s and early 90s population decline, both absolute and proportional, became the basic tendency. This is to be explained by the fact that migrational flows of Russians into Central Asia came to an end, as well as by the universal decline in birth-rate amongst the European population. At the end of the 80s these factors were joined by others: a sharp deterioration in the economic and political situation, and inter-ethnic conflicts generated by the disintegration of the Soviet Union. The declaration of independence by the Central Asian republics, the intensification of inter-ethnic tension and the civil war in Tajikistan have resulted in a new phenomenon: the migration of the Russian population of Central Asia back to the Russian Federation. Today the main factor determining the dynamic of demographic change in Central Asia is the high birth-rate of the native peoples - around 3% per annum i.e. five times higher than in Russia and the Baltic states.

Cultural and Linguistic Aspects of Russification

The Russification of Central Asia was a process that took place on many different fronts. The demographic aspect was only one part of that process - albeit an important one; no less important were cultural and linguistic aspects. The most conspicuous example of this kind of Russification is that offered by the Uzbek language, which is the most important literary language in Central Asia. In the period from the time of Central Asia's joining Russia to the October Revolution of 1917 the Uzbek language was penetrated by approximately 2% of words of Russian origin, and by 1940 more than 15% of words in Uzbek were borrowings from Russian[33]. By the time the Soviet Union disintegrated the number of such borrowings had grown even larger. A similar process occurred with the Tajik, Kazakh, Turkmen and Kyrgyz languages. These languages were much affected by the transition first from the Arabic alphabet to the Latin, then to the Russian. Even more far-reaching, however, were the consequences of the substitution of Russian for native languages in state institutions, in the press, in science, culture, art, educational establishments and in the army. The swift advance of Russification in the cultural and linguistic spheres slowed down development of local languages and even led to part of the native population of Central Asia forgetting their native tongue. In Kazakhstan, for example, 40% of Kazakhs no longer speak Kazakh[34] - whilst, as President Nazarbaev has declared, 'The whole of Kazakhstan speaks Russian, including 99% of Kazakhs'[35]. At the same time, however, the rapid spread of use of the Russian language played an important positive role in making the local population better educated and more cultured, and in stimulating the appearance of a thriving local intelligentsia. It should also be noted that the native population was never compelled to learn or use the Russian language, even if various economic, social and cultural factors under Soviet rule made the ability to speak Russian highly desirable. The general cultural and linguistic situation throughout Central Asia made it impossible for those who did not speak Russian properly to receive higher education, or to get a good job in state and party institutions; whilst ignorance of the Russian language, especially amongst the young of the rural regions of less russified republics - Tajikistan, for example - doomed people to the position of unskilled workers. Central Asians called up for military service and not knowing Russian were immediately assigned to special construction battalions where, for the entire length of their service, they would not once have an opportunity to hold a weapon in their hands. In education and science the Russian language held all the top positions. In the majority of higher-educational establishments teaching was conducted in Russian, and teachers and the majority of students were either Russian or Russian-speaking. Teaching materials and academic publications - at any rate the more serious and better-quality amongst them - were published in Russian. Even after the Central Asian republics had declared independence, and when the native languages had replaced Russian as the official state language, the situation changed slowly. According to statistics for 1994, for example, 78% of students and 57% of school-children in Kazakhstan are taught only in Russian[36]. As earlier, the professional training of Russian specialists is held in high regard. The Central Asian media has more than once admitted that the professional level of native specialists is noticeably lower than that of Russian specialists[37]. And in the mass consciousness of the native Central Asian population knowledge of Russian has always been associated with a high level of education and culture and with increased chances of attaining a higher position in society, without any need to sacrifice traditional values. This explains why the native population was eager to send its children to Russian schools and did everything it could to encourage their coming into contact with the Russian language and culture. In such conditions it is hardly surprising that the majority of Russian and Russian-speaking citizens speak the native language either poorly or not at all. For this reason the new laws, adopted in the Central Asian republics after the disintegration of the Soviet Union and making native languages the official languages of these republics, have put the Russian-speaking population in a difficult position. There can be no doubt that these laws represent an attempt by native nationalists not so much to drive out the Russian language and Russian culture, as to force out the Russian population itself from the positions it holds in the highest economical and political circles in those republics. At the present time the enforcement of these laws has been either suspended or postponed, in recognition of the uniquely important role played by Russians in all spheres of life. In the future, execution of such laws will reflect the political orientation of the Central Asian republics and the way that things develop in Russia itself. But in any case, we can detect a clear desire on the part of the republics to use legislation to halt the far-reaching Russification of Central Asia.

Russification is Bearable, Sovietization is Unendurable

Until the 1980s the influx of Russians into Central Asia and the growing role of Russian language and culture did not call forth feelings of hostility or discontent amongst the majority of the native population of the Central Asian republics - a fact which is to be attributed to the huge positive contribution made by Russians to the rapid economic, social and cultural renaissance of the region. In an attempt to turn Central Asia into a window advertising the achievements of socialism amongst the Afro-Asian peoples, and at the same to offer affirmative proof of Lenin's doctrine of the possibility of a transition from feudalism to socialism with no intermediate stage of capitalism, the Soviet government invested colossal sums of money in the development of the Central Asian republics, redistributing the state budget in favour of this region. Even the serious economic errors made by the central and local planning organizations could not take away from the major advances made here in all spheres of life during the Soviet period. In analyzing the Russification of Central Asia we should not make the mistake of confusing it with the forcible sovietization of the region, a parallel process which from the very beginning evoked a generally negative response amongst the native population. In the consciousness of the Central Asian peoples sovietization was associated with forcible collectivization, a policy which struck a hard blow to the region's agriculture and doomed a considerable part of the peasantry to suffering and death from starvation. In

Kazakhstan alone more than a third of the Kazakh population (1.5 million) died from starvation during collectivization at the beginning of the 1930s[38].

Sovietization also struck a hard blow to native religious feeling. Sovietization meant not only the forced secularization of all spheres of life, as under the Kemalists in Turkey, but militant atheism and an open struggle with Islam as with an ideological rival. In the eyes of the creative intelligentsia sovietization meant the banning of many of the most important national works of literature of the past on grounds of their 'class' or 'nationalistic' character; it also meant being forced to portray all aspects of life according to principles of class consciousness and the principle of 'socialist realism'. Sovietization presupposed a blind subjection to central power, and the conversion of the whole region into an adjunct of the unwieldy and poorly-organized central economic mechanism. Sovietization meant the falsification of the history of the Central Asian peoples, the introduction of stern censorship of all forms of intellectual activity, the merciless suppression of national and religious movements together with any kind of heterodoxy whatsoever. Sovietization was hated; Russification was endured.

The first anti-Russian steps in Central Asia started to occur only in the second half of the 1980s, and were a response to Gorbachev's attempts to limit corruption and the influence of clan and mafia bands amongst the local party nomenclature. This was perceived by high-ranking party functionaries as an infringement of the rules of the game - rules which had been drawn up during the years of the Brezhnev regime, when in exchange for submission and deference in the oriental style, the centre preferred not to interfere in the internal affairs of the Central Asian governments. This policy of 'non-interference' was adhered to despite the continual flow of complaints to Moscow from members of the ordinary population and rank-and-file communists against the corruption and wide-spread abuses perpetrated by members of the local leadership. According to these unwritten rules, the Central Asian ruling elite was given freedom to do as it pleased at home, in return for which it would not press for increased representation in the central organs of power and would take no part in the struggle for power in the centre. Gorbachev, though, also had personal motives for making administrative changes in Central Asia: he intended to replace officials from Brezhnev's circle with people devoted personally to himself. Sensing danger, the local leaders began to play - not openly, of course - the nationalistic card, expressing discontent at Russian and central interference in the internal affairs of the Central Asian republics. The most celebrated and sensational manifestations of their discontent were the demonstrations and disturbances organized by the Kazakhs in Alma Ata in December 1986 as a sign of protest against the removal of Brezhnev's favourite, D. Kunaev, from the post of first secretary of the Communist Party of Kazakhstan and his replacement with G. Kolbin, a Russian by birth. The Kazakh demonstrations were anti-Russian in character and were the first open action of a mass nature, in Soviet times, against the Russification of Kazakhstan. Further proof of the existence of an anti-Russian feeling was the so-called 'Uzbek case', work on which had begun during the short-lived reign of Andropov in 1983. At the heart of this case, also known as 'the cotton case', was a massive fraud linked to supply of cotton and involving, as it transpired, most of the Uzbek party leadership during the rule of First Secretary Raschidov. Hundreds of people were arrested and convicted; many committed suicide; others, such as Raschidov himself, died suddenly in mysterious circumstances. The Central Committee of the Communist Party of the Soviet Union resolved to 'reinforce' its personnel in the republics and, in order to 'restore the region to health', sent to Uzbekistan a large number of Party and economic officials from the centre[39]. Gorbachev's attempts to intervene actively in Uzbek affairs, however, led to an outburst of nationalism among the general public of Uzbekistan, which for the first time expressed its displeasure at the centre's assumption of role of guardian, and began to discuss the Russification of Uzbekistan. Gorbachev's new Central Asian policy was a hopeless failure: it succeeded merely in provoking local nationalism, a phenomenon aggravated by a universal deterioration in the economic situation and a weakening of central power. The rapid disintegration of the Soviet Union also produced changes in the policy priorities of the Central Asian leadership: opposition to Russification was replaced by the search for a new ideological conception and new donor-allies. Poorly-disguised nationalist slogans have now been taken up by the opposition nationalist movements, whilst the former communist leadership now defends the existing political and ethnic status quo in Central Asia today.

Challenges Faced by the Russians

After the disintegration of the Soviet Union the peoples of the former empire experienced the tragic consequences of Soviet national policy-making. Affected most of all, though, were the Russian people itself. More than 25 million Russians found themselves outside the borders of the Russian Federation; approximately 11 million of these were in Central Asia. What is to be the fate of the Russian population of this region? Far from being of concern merely to Russians, the answer to this question will to no small extent decide the future of the new Central Asian states. For the foreseeable future the Russian Federation will be in no condition to take back the entire mass of its nationals, and for this reason any proposal (from whatever source) aimed at returning these Russians to Russia is irresponsible and unreal. On the other hand, Russians continue to make up a significant percentage of the overall population and to play an important role in the economy of the region; they remain an important factor capable of influencing the future development of the new states. Nevertheless, the position and influence of the Russians in the various Central Asian republics is by no means identical, and for this reason their various futures differ too. From this point of view the whole region can be divided into two groups of states: Kazakhstan and Kyrgyzstan, on the one hand; Uzbekistan, Turkmenistan and Tajikistan, on the other. In the first group above the high percentage of Russians in the overall population holds a controlling influence over all spheres of life and will not permit these states to put into action policies contrary to their or Russia's interests. It was in Kazakhstan that the process of Russification went furthest of all; Kazakhstan is the largest republic in the region in terms of territorial size, as well as the richest (from the point of view of raw materials), and the republic with the most developed economy. Here Russians make up almost half the overall population, if taken together with the Russian-speaking population. Kazakhstan has for a long time been part of the Russian Federation in all but name and the state's declaration of independence does nothing to change this on a practical level, except in so far as from the point of view of foreign policy it gives Russia an important voice at conferences between the Central Asian and Islamic states. Only the cautious policy pursued by President Nursultan Nazarbaev, together with a lack of interest (so far!) on the part of Russia, has kept the Russian population of the republic from openly uniting with the Russian Federation, a development which the Kazakhs would be unable to prevent. Kazakhstan is perhaps the only republic in the region whose future, whatever course it takes, will be directly linked with Russia. Nazarbaev himself was principally opposed to the disintegration of the Soviet Union and supported Gorbachev unwaveringly in his unsuccessful attempts to save the disintegrating super power. Slightly less clear is the future of Kyrgyzstan, which is second only to Kazakhstan in extent of Russification. Here Russians make up almost a quarter of the population - or about a half, if taken together with the other Russian-speaking inhabitants of the republic. Like the Kazakhs, the Kyrgyz were until recent times almost all nomads; they inhabit mainly the rural areas of the republic, whilst the cities, industry, education, science and culture are in the hands of the Russians. In Bishkek (formerly Frunze), the capital of the Kyrgyzstan, the Kyrgyz are heavily outnumbered, forming a mere fifth of the city's overall population. This Central Asian republic has possibly more scope for political manoeuvre than Kazakhstan, bearing in mind the smaller proportion of Russians amongst its population and the considerably smaller strategic significance it has for Russia. At the same time, however, Kyrgyzstan will be forced, whatever turn events take, to pay close consideration to the interests of both its own Russian population and Russia, and, in the event of a victory of centripetal forces and the restoration of the union in a new form, will become one of its first members. Asker Akaev, the first Kyrgyz president, was a scientist who lived for many years in Leningrad, and in his education, academic career and political views was close to the democratic movement in Russia. Like Nazarbaev, he was well-known for his pro-Russian orientation and, together with the Kazakh president, was Russia's closest partner at all internal and international meetings. The dominance of the Russian-speaking populations in Kazakhstan and Kyrgyzstan, together with the traditionally weak influence of Islam on the natives of these republics - former nomads, for the most part - considerably limits the scope for action of the Islam fundamentalists. On the other hand, it is precisely these republics that have the strongest democratic and liberal movements, a fact which divides Kazakhstan and Kyrgyzstan from the remaining Central Asian states. The situation with the Kazakh and Kyrgyz nationalist movements is harder to analyze. The local nationalists here are far stronger than the Islamists, although both groups form up on the side of the opposition to the present regimes in Kazakhstan and Kyrgyzstan. The Kazakh nationalist movement, which is secular in character, leans upon the fact that there has already been an independent Kazakh state - that of Alash-Orda, which was proclaimed in December 1917 and, after a short period of existence during the years of the civil war in Russia, liquidated by the Bolsheviks in 1920. The activities of the Kazakh nationalists, if they break out of control of the government, are capable of undermining political stability in the republic, but will not be able to upset the present balance of political power, which is based on the existing ethnic balance.

In distinction to Kazakhstan and Kyrgyzstan, where Russification has either reached a critical point or already surpassed it, in the second group of Central Asian republics the Russian and Russian-speaking populations are far smaller in size. On the eve of the break-up of Soviet Union Russians made up 12% of the overall population in Turkmenistan; 11% in Uzbekistan; 10% in Tajikistan (before the beginning of the civil war 1992-1993)[40]. In these Central Asian republics the position of the Russian inhabitants is appreciably weaker in every respect, and not merely from the point of view of demography. Even before the arrival of the Russians these territories were densely-populated well-developed states with large cities, advanced agriculture and long-established cultural traditions. Unlike the Kazakh and Kyrgyz nomads, who practiced primitive cattle-breeding on a vast and sparsely-populated territory, the Tajik and Uzbek populations were concentrated around the oases of Central Asia, and had a reputation for being hard-working farmers and skilful craftsmen. Amongst them the influence of Islam was traditionally strong. The lack of vacant land, the high density of the population, and the strength of native cultural and religious traditions limited the potential for Russification in these republics. In the third republic, Turkmenistan, Russification was impeded by highly unfavourable climatic conditions which stood in the way of development of agriculture and industry. Like the Kazakhs and Kyrgyz, the tribes of Turkmenistan lived a nomadic life right up to the 20th century, but, unlike the Kazakhs and Kyrgyz, they suffered greatly from a lack of land, since almost the entire territory of Turkmenistan is made up of lifeless deserts unsuitable even for the breeding of pasture cattle. In both groups of Central Asian states similar political processes can be observed - namely, the formation of four basic tendencies: ex-communists, democrats, nationalists and Islamists. In all five republics power rests in the hands of the ex-communists, who often see no reason to conceal their past. Only in Kyrgyzstan did the rule of the former president Akaev have some appearance of being a partnership between the ex-communists and other political forces - although here too the former are clearly the more powerful. The sympathies of the Russian population in this region are divided between two tendencies by no means equal in strength: the former party bureaucracy, in whom they see hope for political stability; and the democratic movements, whose call is for the observance of human rights and for a fight against the local mafia. The astonishingly rapid disintegration of the Soviet Union and the declaration of independence by all the national republics stunned the local Russian population and temporarily paralyzed their political activity. In a flash the

Russian population in Central Asia, instead of being the 'elder brother' and representative of the chief nation in the superstate, became a run-of-the-mill minority amongst peoples who are alien and far-removed from them in language, culture, religion and history. To add insult to injury, Russia itself, in the immediate wake of the collapse of the Soviet Union, took no part either in defending the interests of the Russians in the region or in supervising the return to the Russian Federation of those who wished to do so. There is no doubt, however, that the shock and confusion which seized Russians in the Central Asian republics, and the bitter feeling that they had been betrayed by the Russian leaders, is only a temporary phenomenon; we should expect to see the appearance of movements of political unity amongst the Russians, in response to local nationalism, in regions where the Russian population is strong - in Kazakhstan and Kyrgyzstan, for example. An important role will in all likelihood be played by the former Semirechinsk Cossacks, as the most lively and united group of Russians in Central Asia.

Outbursts of nationalism and Islamic fundamentalism amongst the native peoples, a sharp deterioration in all links with Russia, a catastrophic drop in the standard of living, and - which is most important - the lack of political stability and personal security in conditions where other nationalities predominate has led to the Russian population coming to feel anxiety for its own life and property, and fear for the future. According to figures published in the Russian press, only 8% of the Russian population consider life in Central Asia acceptable[41]. The Central Asian press has confirmed this tendency: if, for example 31% of Kazakhs feel confident in their future, that feeling is shared by only 8% of Russians[42]. All prognoses for the future of the Russian and Russian-speaking populations of Central Asia come down to two possible scenarios. The first of these supposes that centripetal tendencies will once again come to prevail on the territory of the former Soviet Union, leading to the formation of a new unified state. In this case a new regime, most probably of a totalitarian type, will restore to the Russian population the status and position it held before the disintegration of the Soviet Union, whilst using force to suppress all ethno-religious and national conflicts on its territory. The second scenario proceeds from the assumption that the disintegration of the formerly unified superpower is an irreversible fact; return to a centralized state is already impossible; and the Commonwealth of Independent States is a dead-born baby, participation in which is for the former national republics merely a temporary step dictated by political expedience. Under this scenario the position of the Russian population in the Central Asian states will progressively deteriorate because the native population is bound to try to force Russians out of the leading positions they occupy in society and in the economy, and also because of a growth in nationalist and Islamic sentiment. Sooner or later, the Russians will be forced to leave Uzbekistan, Tajikistan and Turkmenistan i.e. the group of Central Asian republics in which Russians make up a relatively small part of the overall population (from 10% to 12%). If failure to produce satisfactory economic results forces the former communist leadership of these states to surrender power to nationalist or Islamic elements, the Russian exodus will turn into a stampede. The accession to power of the nationalists or Islamists will undermine the little remaining political stability in the region and lead inevitably to civil wars and ethnic conflicts. A classic example of such a conflict is the civil war in Tajikistan in 1992 - 1993. Here the former communist leadership, riddled with corruption and generally weak, surrendered power for a short time - not voluntarily, of course - to an ill-assorted coalition of Islamists, nationalists and democrats. The new regime literally choked in a war in which everyone fought against everyone else, which in turn led to the headlong flight of the Russian population, whilst also generating the problem of Tajik refugees in Afghanistan. If there were half a million Russians in Tajikistan before the civil war, Russian experts put the number in 1994 at no more than 80 000[43]. As for the other group of states in this region - i.e. Kazakhstan and Kyrgyzstan - the second scenario could cause an explosion of political and even military activity amongst the large Russian and Russian-speaking populations. This in turn will lead either to the Russians seizing power and to these republics joining the Russian Federation under conditions of compulsion, or to the more Russian parts of the region declaring their own independence, as has already happened with the Pridnestrovskaya Republic in Moldova. In Kazakhstan the most well-developed regions of the north-east are densely-populated with Russians and, in the event of an outbreak of inter-ethnic conflict, could either unite directly with Russia or, as a half-way stage to the latter, declare themselves independent. The situation in Kyrgyzstan is harder to predict; here the problem of the Russian population lies somewhere between the problems of the Russian populations in Kazakhstan and in the other Central Asian republics. The Russian population of Kyrgyzstan is far more numerous and far stronger than in Uzbekistan, Turkmenistan or Tajikistan, and for this reason is unlikely to leave the country of its own free will; on the other hand, its ability to undertake independent and far-reaching political action is as yet unproven.

The Role of the Russian Army

There is one more important factor in Central Asia which gives the Russian population increased influence in the region: the army. Detachments of the former Soviet - now, Russian - army till this day hold key positions in Tajikistan and Kyrgyzstan; the former communist leadership has so far refrained from raising the question of their withdrawal from these Central Asian states, looking upon them - as well it might - as a guarantee of political stability and military balance in the region. For its part, the Russian army prefers to keep a neutral position in local political conflicts and uses force only in exceptional circumstances: either for self-defence, or to protect the Russian population, as happened during the civil war in Tajikistan.

Following the disintegration of the Soviet Union the Western and Israeli press carried a lot of speculation regarding the possibility of Turkmenistan, Uzbekistan and Tajikistan possessing tactical atomic weapons; there was even talk that Iranian secret-agents had managed to buy and transport to Iran several tactical nuclear war-heads. These rumours had their foundation in the realities of the time - namely, the drop in discipline and morality in the Soviet army during the disintegration of the Soviet Union, and the state of anarchy which obtained over a vast territory following the unsuccessful coup attempt of August 1991. The widespread incidence of illegal sale of weapons and the almost unchecked activities of the mafia gave rise in the West and in Israel to fears that the Islamic fundamentalists could exploit the situation of general chaos and confusion to obtain an atomic bomb with which to neutralize Israel's nuclear potential and blackmail the West. The extent to which this was taken seriously at that time by the West was proved by the scandal which broke out at the beginning of 1993 in Poland, when the former Minister of Defence accused the Polish President, Lech Walensa, of giving orders, during the collapse of the Soviet Union, for the illegal purchase of a small number of atomic weapons for the use of the Polish army. Regardless of the question of the truth of these claims - which, incidentally, were refuted by the Polish president - they demonstrate how great was the temptation amongst certain countries and extremist movements to obtain nuclear weapons, and how great was the fear in the West and in Israel that such weapons would in fact fall into the hands of extremists in the conditions of anarchy and general chaos generated by the collapse of the Soviet Union. The American and Israeli intelligence services went to great lengths to check the truth of these rumours of the illegal supply of atomic war-heads to Iran through Central Asia, but were unable to find conclusive proof. For example, Uri Sagi, the head of Israeli military intelligence, declared that 'the media sensations regarding supply of nuclear weapons to Iran from the former USSR have no solid foundation whatsoever. At any rate, I have no such proof'[44]. Sagi emphasized that according to the information at his disposal 'Russia is exercising satisfactory control over its nuclear potential. Some leakage of materials or information is possible. But as for someone stealing three bombs and supplying them to Iran, that I cannot believe, it's impossible'[45].

There is good reason to suppose that if for a short period there were tactical nuclear weapons in Central Asia, then they were under the full and absolute control of the Russian army, which would have despatched them to Russia in good time.

Pending Russia's New Policy

In considering possible directions for the future of Central Asia, we should emphasize that the decisive factor here will be the state of the economy - and not, however paradoxical this may seem, the state of the local Central Asian economy so much as the state of the Russian one. The fate of the Central Asian republics depends to a large extent on Russia's policy-making in the region, whilst Russia's policy priorities are determined by her economic interests. The first attempts of Yeltsin's reformers to switch in a short space of time from a planned socialist economy to a capitalist market-based economic system led to a sharp fall in production, to hyperinflation and a catastrophic decline in living standards. Utter anarchy in the economy and the unprecedented social stratification and impoverishment of the population forced Yeltsin at the end of 1992 to sacrifice, under pressure from the conservative majority in parliament, his chief reformer, Yegor Gaydar, and appoint a new premier-minister of a more moderate tendency; this was Victor Chernomyrdin, who, in spite of holding views opposed to those of Gaydar, nevertheless did not abandon the path of reform. The defeat of the democratic reformers in the parliamentary elections of 1993, however, compelled Chernomyrdin's government to slow down the pace of reform, and to renounce some reforms altogether.

This first, unsuccessful, experience of economic reform in Russia, together with the state of shock suffered by the economies of the former communist block in Eastern Europe, has shown that, in contrast to the smooth transition from capitalism to socialism engineered by the Marxists, the reverse journey, as yet uncharted by anyone, is likely to take far longer than was earlier supposed. It would indeed be naive to think that the development of a modern capitalist system of production and of the brand of Western democracy which is its product, a development which in the West took a whole century, could be accomplished by Russia and the countries of Eastern Europe in the space of a few years. In this respect all the precocious plans for transition to a market economy in 100, 300 or 500 days worked out in Russia even as the Soviet Union was still falling apart, look at the very least not at all serious. It should also be borne in mind that the experience of economic development gained in Eastern European states of relatively small size - such as Chekhia or even Poland - which set out on the path of reform at an earlier date, cannot always be applied to a country as vast as Russia. Russian politicians and economists long underestimated the successful reforms in China, where the Communist Party retained control whilst many sectors of the economy effected a smooth and shock-less transition to a market system, efficient use was made of private Chinese and foreign capital, and the general standard of living rose significantly i.e. Gorbachev's 'perestroika' was realized, but without 'glasnost'. A justification for the difficult path taken by Russia via 'decommunization' may be found in the intransigence of the Communist Party apparat - whose position, compared to that of its Chinese counterpart, was quite uncompromising: Party officials did everything they could to slow down the course of reforms and even organized a coup in August 1991. The failure of the reformers to create a capitalist-based market economy and Western-type system of democratic institutions, and to prevent a deepening of the economic crisis in Russia in 1992 - 1994, have made society look for alternative economic and political solutions. At the present time there are three such alternatives. The first is that offered by the new communist opposition, which gradually reformed after the rout of the old Communist Party and grows stronger with every new mistake made by the reformers. Although the communists press for the restoration of the old Soviet Union and for socialism, they have no desire to return to the absolute dictatorship of the Party over all spheres of public life, to the policy of repressions practiced between 1930 - 1950, or to the disreputable stagnation of 1970 - 1990. At the same time, however, their proposed exit from the crisis consists of nothing more than various liberalized variations on the traditional Marxist-Leninist programme for social development, the strong point of which is the degree of social security it promises the general public. The reborn Russian communist party is as yet too weak and too badly-organized to pose a serious threat to the new ruling powers. The second alternative is that offered by supporters of the traditional Russian national ideology, a group which incudes both Russian patriotic parties and nationalist parties of various hues (e.g. Zhirinovskiy's Liberal Democratic Party). These parties are united by the idea of restoring to Russia its superpower status, although they have differing conceptions of the restored superpower's territorial size: some conceive it as occupying the territory of the former Soviet Union; others, as fitting within the boundaries of a Russian Federation expanded to include the Russian-populated districts of the national republics. Still more contradictory and vague are these parties' social and economic programmes - based on principles which vary from the social-democratic to the neo-conservative, and featuring policies as various as that of active state regulation, at one end of the scale, and the idea of a free market economy, at the other. All these parties and organizations are united by a shared hatred of the old Communist Party, on the one hand, and by opposition to the anti-national - as they see it - course taken by the reformers, on the other.

The third alternative direction amongst the forces of the opposition is the least formalized of the three, and the least ideological, but potentially the strongest. Supporters of this direction are united by the conviction that the reforms have struck a dead-end, that the country is in the process of disintegrating into smaller and smaller territorial and administrative units, and that economic catastrophe and inter-ethnic conflicts have placed under threat the vital interests of the peoples of the former Soviet Union. For this reason they see their main goal as the salvation of the country (not merely Russia) through the establishment of strong rule over the entire territory, forceful elimination of all inter-ethnic conflicts, an efficient system of social security, stabilization of the economy and reprioritization in foreign policy. Amongst the holders of these views are staunch communists, Russian nationalists, and even supporters of the reforms who believe that the only way to save the country and carry out the changes needed is through the imposition of some form or other of totalitarian or authoritarian regime, at any rate for the duration of the transitional period. Opinions such as this are common amongst the army and the security forces, as well as throughout the various different elements of Russian society, where they receive a positive response amongst a population exhausted by economic difficulties. One of the most influential organizations to have taken on board this programme is the Front of National Salvation, a political grouping which gave Yeltsin and his entourage such a fright on its appearance that it was banned immediately after the dissolution of the Russian parliament in October 1993, accused of preparing a coup. The imposition of strong rule, incidentally, is quite possible through constitutional means, given the steady decline of Yeltsin's authority amongst the population, as of that of the reformer-democrats. Moreover, the new Russian constitution adopted in December 1993 gives such sweeping powers to the president as to make the transition to authoritarianism relatively easy.

More complicated is the question of the ideological foundation behind the Russian government and its policy-making in the postcommunist period. If the new regime is forced to stick to the boundaries of the Russian Federation, then there can be no doubt that the dominant ideology will be a form of Russian nationalism with its traditional three hypostases - authoritarianism, national character and orthodoxy. In this event, however, there will be inevitable conflicts with the countries of the 'near abroad' on account of the interests of the multi-million Russian population living in those states, as well as because of borders arbitrarily established during Soviet times. This course of events would bring peace and stability to not one of the peoples that inhabit the vast Euro-Asian territory of the former Soviet Union. The alternative, a new authoritarian government whose authority would spread over all, or a majority of, the former Soviet republics, is much to be preferred from the point of view of providing political and economic stability, and would be capable of resolving the existing inter-ethnic and territorial conflicts within the framework of a unified central state. However, the Russian national idea is not a candidate for becoming the new shared ideology which will re-cement the multinational superpower. It is to be regretted that neither during the disintegration of the Soviet Union, nor afterwards, has there appeared a single ideological conception, alternative both to Marxist-Leninism and to multi-hued nationalism, which would breathe new life into a multinational Union. At the end of the 80s Gorbachev made an unsuccessful attempt to renovate and reanimate the lifeless dogmata of Marxism-Leninism, in which almost everyone had stopped believing, but which people continued to respect through force of inertia or external compulsion. Taking over from Gorbachev, Yeltsin and his democrat-reformers were acting in an ideological vacuum, in as much as they had nothing to offer but the values of the consumer society and western parliamentarism. The former national republics were engulfed by a wave of long pent-up nationalism, which first broke free, then seized power, and then either generated numerous inter-ethnic conflicts or degenerated into a vulgar chauvinism towards ethnic minorities. However, economic requirements and the universal desire for political stability throughout the huge expanse of

Euro-Asia cry out for the restoration of a single and necessarily multinational state, which will need a new ideological framework and foundation. As Francis Fukuyama has so rightly stressed, nations strive to live for something more than consumer prosperity and universal values. For reasons of a historical nature, the level of ideologization in Russia has always been higher than in other European countries, which is why the continued existence of the ideological vacuum which formed after the unexpected and spontaneous de-communization occurring in August 1991, could have dangerous consequences not merely for the Russian Federation itself, but also for the former national republics. The new Russian leadership which will replace the democrat-reformers will face a difficult dilemma: either to try to modernize the Marxist-Leninist model of a multinational state, adding to it in the future elements of social democracy (socialism 'with a human face') such as pluralism and the mixed economy; or to return to the pre-Revolutionary traditional conception of a Russian multinational state. Neither conception can be put into practice without the use, or at least the threat, of force - since Russia has both a lack of a democratic tradition and an abundance of explosive material capable of fuelling national and territorial conflicts. In the present situation in Russia pluralist democracy and economic liberalism will constitute no threat to the integrity of the state only if they are controlled and directed from above. This raises the question of how such control is to be limited and how long such control is to be continued on the way to a democratic market-economy state in the western sense of that term. A lengthy transitional period with an authoritarian-style government and periodic use of force is inevitable and necessary in the postcommunist stage of Russian history. The western form of democracy so desired by the Russian reformers is the result of a lengthy historical evolution supported by a long-standing democratic tradition and liberal, capitalism-oriented market economy. The political history of many countries of the 'Third World' furnishes clear proof that the lack of these vital historical, social and economic factors deprives the western type of parliamentary democracy of any chance of survival, even if assistance is available from the West. There is no reason to think that Russia could prove an exception to this rule.

Nor is there any reason to doubt that there will be significant changes in Russia's foreign policy. The 'Atlanticism' - i.e. orientation towards the USA and the countries of Western Europe - characteristic of Yeltsin's government in the period immediately following the disintegration of the Soviet Union, must inevitably give way to 'Euro-Asianism' - a policy oriented on the Near and Middle East, on Asia as a whole and on the countries of Eastern and South-eastern Europe. Russia's geographical position and the significant proportion of Turkish and Islamic peoples amongst its population are both arguments for such a development. Moreover, Russia does not have the necessary economic muscle and prosperity to become a member of the elite Atlantic Club - which it has been invited to take part in only because of its military might, and then only in the role of passive observer. From this point of view the hasty steps taken by President Yeltsin and his Minister of Foreign Affairs, Kozyrev, to make drastic cuts in Russia's military potential in response to feelings of euphoria at the end of the cold war, take insufficient account of the country's national interests; Russia became a great power, and for the meantime remains one, largely due to military might. Russian history over the course of the last centuries shows that economically Russia was always weaker than its main rivals in the West and made up for its economic weakness only by being militarily strong. The sharp reduction of the Russian and American military potentials will hit hardest at Russia's political interests, in as much as America's economic might in any case guarantees it the status of a superpower, which cannot be said of Russia. For this reason the future postcommunist government of Russia will undoubtedly put the brakes on the conversion of military industry begun by the reformers, and may even try to change the existing Russo-American agreement on nuclear weapons reduction. The first signs of a hardening of Russia's foreign policy were already noticeable in the wake of the defeat of the democrat-reformers in the parliamentary elections of December 1993. From this moment onwards the 'Euro-Asian' accent in Russian policy-making became noticeably stronger.

After the collapse of the Soviet Union analysts in the Russian Ministry of Foreign Affairs advised concentration on rapprochement with the USA and the countries of Western Europe; at the same time they recommended that Russia make haste to slip the heavy burden of the backward Central Asian republics, states which, in their opinion, could only make the course of economic reform more difficult and hold back the second westernization of Russia (the first being that conducted by Peter I). It is possible that from the theoretical point of view this advice was justified, but its authors nevertheless failed to take into account Russia's geopolitical position and the Russian population in Central Asia, whilst clearly overestimating the likely scale of financial and technological aid on offer from the West. However, the most important factor, and one which is capable of making Russia's postcommunist government choose the Euro-Asian accent in foreign policy, will be the millions of Russians who live outside the Russian Federation - especially since the former national republics are as yet far from institutionalization of a liberal democracy based on a respect for human rights. The tragic example of the civil war in Yugoslavia in 1991 - 1994 has exerted a moderating influence on the temptation to use force to protect the civil rights of Russians living in the states of the 'near abroad'. But the deterioration of the position of the Russian population in those countries, and the threat posed to their lives and property - a threat which has already been made real in Tajikistan - will in any case force the Russian government to concentrate on a Euro-Asian policy and consider the use of force. There is no doubt that post-communist Russia's foreign policy will move closer and closer to the traditional Russian policy-making of the 18th and 19th centuries with its unchanging and difficult 'eastern question'.

Chapter Three

THE AWAKENING OF CENTRAL ASIAN ISLAM

During the long years of Soviet rule, the Muslims of the USSR were the silent, submissive face of an Islam whose passivity surprised and disappointed many observers. In comparison with the militant and dynamic Islam of the Third World, Soviet Muslims seemed to have become nothing more than an inert appendage to the ideological apparat of the Communist Party. The Soviet Union had the fifth largest Muslim population after Indonesia, Pakistan, India and Bangladesh; yet it remained a blank spot on the political map of Islam. It seemed that Soviet ideologues had in fact succeeded in creating their much-proclaimed synthesized 'homo sovieticus', a creature in whom all national and religious bonds had supposedly been eliminated.

'Neglected' Islam first delivered a reminder of its existence in the period of reform initiated by Mikhail Gorbachev, when political liberalization led to an increase in religious activity. On the eve of the disintegration of the USSR the country's Muslim population numbered 56 million, i.e. 20% of the overall population. Almost 70% of all Soviet Muslims lived in Central Asia. Ethnically, an absolute majority of Central Asian Muslims are of Turkic origin, and, of the major Central Asian peoples, only the Tadjiks are Farsi-speaking. From a chronological point of view, the population of Central Asia was the first of the peoples of the former USSR who are presently Muslim to adopt Islam; they did so during the Arab conquest of the region in the 7th to 8th centuries. The Islamization of Central Asia, however, was completed only later, in the 9th century. Moreover, the Arabs managed to Islamize the local populations using mainly economic rather than military means.   From the very beginning Central Asian Islam was distinguished by two features: 1) the large number of pre-Islamic beliefs and cults which made their way into the local ariety of Islam; 2) the special role played by the unofficial clergy in the religious life of the region.

The Central Asian Clergy

In Central Asia, as in most Muslim countries, there were for a long time two categories of Muslim clergy. The first category - the official clergy - consisted of clergymen holding an official position - sheikhul'islams, kadi, raises, muddarrises, imams, etc; these were supported by numerous fanatical mullah-bashi (i.e. the students of madrasahs), and constituted a highly unified corporation with a strong influence over all social groups amongst the population. In Bukhara, for example, even the emir was unable to put his decisions into practice without first receiving the approval of a member of the higher clergy: for this reason the emirs generally tried not to come into conflict with the official clergy. The Bukhara clergy was always able to count on support from amongst the large numbers of students of madrasahs - mullah-bashi. The latter were also divided into groups, of which there were two main ones. The first

group consisted of children of officials from Bukhara and the surrounding area; the second, of those who had come from elsewhere
(mainly from Eastern Bukhara). The more important officials usually tried to secure the backing of the muddarrises, in as far as
the latter had the support of the mullah-bashi and their authority
could be counted on to strengthen the officials' position. At the
end of the 19th century the city of Bukhara had a population of 80
to 100 thousand, and contained 365 mosques and 103 madrasahs
attended by 15 to 20 thousand mullah-bashi[46]. The economic influence of the Muslim clergy was especially powerful. In the Emirate
of Bukhara, for example, at least 25% of all land under cultivation
- and in the khanate of Khiva, as much as 40% - belonged to Muslim
institutions (waqf). The Muslim clergy played a less important role
only in the Khokand khanate.

The second category of Muslim clergy in Central Asia was made
up of dervish sheikhs - ishans. The latter took up a position opposed to that of the official clergy, and preached asceticism as
well as many beliefs which were animistic or pre-Islam. The ishans
had a broad network of dervish-murid organizations embracing
all sections of the population; the more important of these organizations even had the support of the Bukhara emirs and Khiva
khans. All these dervish organizations traced their origins back
to the Sufistic orders which had spread widely not just in Central
Asia, but throughout the Muslim East. Sufistic ideology and ritual, as is well-known, had close links with ancient local cults as
well as with elements from various philosophical systems (panthe-
ism, in particular). Sufism's syncretist ideology gave its followers
the opportunity to accept whatever aspect of the faith most fitted in with their world outlook and level of culture. This explains
why Sufism's ideology had equal popularity in Central Asia both
amongst the aristocracy and amongst the simple people. Whilst

keeping intact its general content, Sufism subsequently spilt into a number of different orders and branches. The branch with the largest following on the territory of modern Uzbekistan was the order of Naqshbandi, founded by the Bukharan sufi Bagoutdin Naqshband in the 14th century. Also popular - especially in the Fergana Valley - was the order of Kadyr, founded in the 12th century by Abdulkadyr Gilyani. The order of Kubraviya, named after its founder Nadzhmeddin Kubr (12th century) had a particularly strong following in Khorezm. In the north of Uzbekistan the dominant order was that of Yasaviya, founded in the 12th century by Ahmed Yasevi, who was responsible for spreading Islam amongst the nomads. In the 16th century the order of Hodzhagon gained in influence in Bukhara; to this order belonged the famous dzhuibar hodzhis, who had strengthened their position during the rule of Abdul-khan of the Sheibanid dynasty, and who preserved their influence over the emirs of Bukhara until the very end of the Bukhara emirate[47].

Each of these orders was headed by descendants of its founder (pirzoda). Some Sufi communities were headed by ishans who received the right to mentorship (irshad) either by descent or with the blessing of their own mentor. Everyone entering an order became a Murid, delivering himself wholly into the power of a particular ishan. The murid renounced his own free will, and undertook to keep no secrets from his mentor whilst at the same time keeping the latter's secrets religiously. Murids also engaged to hand over every year a part of their income to their ishan.

Notable amongst the dervish orders of Central Asia was the organization of the begging dervishes - the Kalyandars, - who lived on charity. Considering their founder to be Bagoutdin Naqshband, the dervishes of this order set up closed communities in which begging was a hereditary profession providing sufficient income to give the Kalyandar and his family a comfortable existence. Folk legend dates the order's foundation to the 18th century, attributing it to a certain sheikh Safa, who lived in Samarkand. The head of the Kalyandars was a descendant of Safa, who called him 'tyurya' or 'Sir'. The Central Asian Kalyandars did not practise the usual kind of 'zikr', nor did they work themselves up into a condition of ecstasy. In place of the latter rituals, they held, usually in the mornings, special prayer gatherings in the house of the tyurya and under his supervision, at which they chanted religious verse and prayers in unison.

The Influence of Pre-Islamic Cults and Beliefs

By the beginning of the 20th century the link between the dervish organizations and their original Sufistic orders was recognizable only with difficulty: Sufism had degenerated into Ishanism, and every ishan of any reputation became in time the founder of a separate order. On the other hand, Ishanism, as a Central Asian variety of Sufism, had absorbed a large number of pre-Islamic beliefs and elements of ancient cults. A typical pre-Islamic belief was the widespread respect which was given to fire. People believed that fire should not be put out by blowing, and that nothing unclean should be poured onto the ashes; at festivals it was the practice to light fires and jump through them (this was regarded as purifying); newly-wed brides were also led around the fire. Traces of ancient beliefs can also be seen in the cosmogonic notions which are to this day common amongst the Tadjiks. Typical are, for example, the notion of thunder as the deity Tundur, who appears in the form of an old man or old woman beating the dust out of his or her fur coat; the idea of the clouds as cows; the idea of the rainbow as Rustam's bow (in Islam the place of the latter was taken by the holy men Hasan and Husayn). Particularly strong was a belief in various magical actions as capable of bringing good to a man or of inflicting harm on his enemy.

The cult of mazars or venerable places is widely practised to this day. Such places are generally the tombs of Muslim holy men, but can be other objects which are in some way or other remarkable - trees, large stones, caves, springs. One of the most venerable mazars, and one which attracts a large number of pilgrims, is the grave of Kussam ibn Abbas, cousin of Muhammad; situated in Samarkand, this is known as Shakhi-Zinda ('Living tsar'). According to legend, Kussam ibn Abbas, who had been killed in a fight between the Muslims and the local population, descended under the ground, bearing in his hands his own severed head. The irrigation ditch flowing near the mazar is to this day called Obi-Maschad ('The river of the place of the martyr's death'). Various details in the legend and the place-name point to the cult of the Muslim saint overlaying an older cult - the ancient cult, common in ancient Central Asia, of the god who dies and is born again. One of the most venerable mazars in the city of Bukhara is the mausoleum of Ismail Samanid. According to a popular superstition, the king of Samanid, though dead, continues to engage in state business. There is a specially-made crack in his tomb through which believers post their petitions. No less famous are mazars in other parts of Central Asia - the mausoleum of Hodji Ahmed Yasavi in Kazakhstan, and, in Kyrgyzstan, the Suleyman mountain near the town of Osh. Several mazars are located in the vicinity of healing springs, (e.g. the mazar of Hazret-Ayub in Jalalabad), or in areas favoured with an outstanding natural climate (e.g. the mazar of Shakhimardan in Fergana). The keepers of the mazars - called sheikhs - have always lived on the offerings brought by believers who come seeking help. There are particularly many sheikhs in mazars such as Shakhi-Zinda. Far from remaining constant, the number of mazars has steadily increased as a result of the appearance of new mazars, including in many cases the tombs of famous ishans. The cult of the mazar is deeply rooted in other ancient cults. Many mazars had been places of worship in pre-Islamic times; the legends about them are a complex conglomerate of Muslim and pre-Islamic elements which have intertwined with each other in a whimsical way. In spite of this, veneration for mazars has become a firm part of Central Asian Islam and has the backing of the official clergy. In pre-Soviet and especially in Soviet times only a very few could make the pilgrimage to Mecca (hadj); for this reason up till the 1970s the Muslim clergy in Central Asia used to recommend that hadj be replaced by visits made to local holy mazars. It is interesting to note that the Muslim Spiritual Board of Central Asia and Kazakhstan, far from speaking out against the practice of making pilgrimages to mazars, in fact at many such sacred places actually supported people to attend the sites. It is only in recent times, and especially following the break up of the USSR, that the Central Asian Muslim religious authorities and authorities at mosques have started to speak out both against the cult of mazars and against any comparison of visits to local sacred places with the hadj to Mecca. This has a lot to do with the fact that Muslim fundamentalists, who take a confrontational attitude to the official clergy, have started to make active use of the cult of mazars in order to strengthen their influence amongst the population.

Central Asian Islam has also taken over the ancient cult of the chiltanis. The latter are anonymous just men who are selected from amongst the living, forty at a time, and who, whilst continuing their former lives, exert an influence on the course of events and save people from disaster. Also Islamized were the ancient

Central Asian cults of female divinities; the latter are now well-known as Muslim holy women - Bibi-seshanbi (Lady Tuesday) and Bibi-Mushkilkusho (Lady Who Resolves Difficulties).

Another example of the Islamization of ancient Central Asian cults and rites is the holiday of the vernal equinox - Navruz ('New Day'). This holiday was first celebrated by Farsi-speaking peoples in the 9th - 10th centuries B.C, and was linked to the solar calendar. The Muslim calendar is lunar. The Arabs who brought Islam to Central Asia very quickly realized the enormous importance of Navruz for the local population, and accordingly gave the holiday their encouragement - whilst imparting to it an Islamic character. The Islamization of Navruz is evident in particular in changes made to the holiday's ritual symbology: wine, which was disapproved of by the Shari'at, was excluded from use at the holiday, as were candles, which symbolized worship of fire. Subsequently, Muslim ideologues hit upon an important coincidence: it so happened that the day marked by Navruz was the day when imam Ali came to power in the Caliphate. Following the establishment of Soviet rule in Central Asia, the communists made frequent attempts to forbid the celebration of Navruz out of fear of its religious character. Popular pressure, however, forced them to back down, and, on the eve of the break up of the USSR, they went so far as to declare the day a public holiday. At the same time, the local authorities continue even now to underline the holiday's pre-Islamic origins and its traditional agricultural character.

The Shiites

There are very few Shiites in Central Asia; approximate estimates put their numbers at no more than 50 - 60 thousand. The Shiites started to appear in Central Asia in the 16th century, at the time when the northern part of Iran suffered systematic raids. This explains why the first Muslim Shiites appeared in Sunnite Central Asia as prisoners of war. They were subsequently joined by Shiites from the city of Merv who had been forcibly resettled on Bukharan territory by Shakh-Murad, the emir of Bukhara. In addition to such resettlement by force there was also a certain amount of voluntary migration of Shiites from the northern regions of Iran and Afghanistan. A further element in the Shiite population of Central Asia consisted of part of the Pamiran peoples of Badakhshan, who profess an Ismailitic form of Shiism.

The Shiites of Central Asia are generally given the name of 'Ironi'. This name is an ethnographic description of the group of which a considerable part was Iranian in origin and which has retained the Shiite faith. Linguistically, the Ironi living in the various parts of Central Asia are divided into Tadjik- and Turkic-speaking peoples. The majority of Tadjik-speaking Shiites live in Bukhara, Darvaz, Kulyab, whilst the Turkic-speaking Shiites are to be found in Samarkand, Dzhizak and Kamashi.

In some cases the old names for certain neighbourhoods serve as an indication of the mixed ethnic origin of the Ironi. In the kishlak of Zirobod, for example - a village whose population is mostly made up of Ironi - the guzar (neighbourhood) of Kypchok takes its name from the kypchaks, immigrants from Afghanistan; whilst the guzar of Buludzh is named after the Beludzhes, who moved here from the town of Kuchan in northern Khorasan. It is worth noting that the ancestors of some of these immigrants (in particular, the Kypchaks, Beludzhes and even the Arabs) were originally Sunnites, but, on settling amongst the Ironi, where they were surrounded by a Shiite population, had by the second generation become Shiites[48].

It should be stressed that the Ironi-Shiites in the past settled in concentrated groups, but not in isolation from the surrounding population. Amongst the Shiites there were many craftsmen; and these were linked with the greater part of the Sunnite population (Uzbeks and Tadjiks) by the fact of their shared profession. Also to a large extent responsible for bringing Shiites and Sunnites closer together was the administrative role which had been assigned the Ironi in Bukhara from as far back as the rule of the first emirs of the Mangyt dynasty. Under Daniyalbiy (1758 - 1785), for instance, the Shiite Davlet-biy was appointed Grand Vizier 'Kushbegi'. The armed guard of the rulers of Bukhara was largely made up of Ironi slaves. During the reign of the last emir of Bukhara not merely the post of Kushbegi, but many other high-ranking posts were filled by Ironi-Shiites. The position of the Shiites in the emirate improved to such an extent that they began to perform their religious rites, or ashuri, not in special rooms (husaynia or husayniyakhona), but in the open air outside the city walls. Such a marked strengthening of the Shiites' influence in the emirate of Bukhara earned the displeasure of the Sunnite clergy, and particularly of the large numbers of those studying in the madrasahs (mullah-bashis). This resulted in January 1910 in an explosion of butcherous violence between the Sunnites and Shiites, following which the opponents of the Shiites, headed by Mir-Burkhanuddin Badriddinov, succeeded in removing the Ironi Astanakul from the post of Kushbegi[49]. An attempt by the Russian political agent in Bukhara to protect the Shiites from pogroms and to punish the initiators of such pogroms had only short-lived success, and was a factor in the intensification of anti-Russian sentiment amongst the Muslim clergy. In Soviet times the existence of the Ironi-Shiites as a distinct ethnographic and religious group in Central Asia was often ignored; alternatively, the Ironi-Shiites were viewed merely from the point of view of ethnology, i.e. as Persians (Iranians). For example, in the census of 1959 the Ironi-Shiites were passed over altogether without mention, whilst in that of 1970 they were marked down only as Iranians (Persians). Moreover, the extent of the Ironi-Shiite population was for various reasons played down: the Tadjik-speaking Ironi of Bukhara were counted as Tadjiks, whilst the Turkic-speaking Ironi of Samarkand were counted as Uzbeks[50]. Whereas under Soviet rule the activities of official Sunnite Islam were subject to restriction and suppression, the religious life of the Central Asian Shiites was altogether paralyzed. Until the disintegration of the USSR the Shiites had not a single working husayniyakhona. The Ashuri - Shiite mysteries dedicated to memories of the death of Husayn, the son of Ali - were celebrated in secret in people's houses. Following the Islamic revolution in Iran in 1978/1979, the Soviet authorities began to look with still greater suspicion upon all religious activity undertaken by the Central Asian Shiites, and suppressed such activity without hesitation. As a result, the Ironi underwent widespread assimilation, merging more and more, in terms of culture and language, with the surrounding Tadjik and Uzbek populations; mixed marriages between Sunnites and Shiites became common. The break-up of the USSR and the reanimation of religious life amongst the Ironi-Shiites halted the process of loss of religious self-identity amongst this group. The future of the group nevertheless remains unclear. The official Sunnite clergy of Central Asia continues to be highly circumspect in its attitude to the growth of activity amongst the Shiites; the same attitude is shown by the ex-communist leadership of the Central Asian republics. Today, as in the past, the Ironi-Shiites take pains to underline that they are much less fanatical in their performance of religious rites than are the Sunnites. Such assertions, though, could well be taken as exemplifying an article from the Shiite code of behaviour - 'takiya', which permits the Shiite to conceal his faith and refrain from carrying out the instructions of the cult if circumstances call for it. On the other hand, the religious tolerance shown by the Central Asian Shiites could just as well be a consequence of the long time they have spent in separation from their native environment and surrounded by people of an alien faith.

Understanding the very small weight possessed by the Shiites amongst the overall Muslim population of Central Asia, the official clergy of Iran prefers not to give them special attention or favour. In the eyes of Iranian fundamentalists, though, the fact that part of the Pamiran peoples in Gorniy Badakhshan (in Tadjikistan) close to the border with Afghanistan are Ismailitic Shiites has very real value. Ismailism was an important factor contributing to the isolation of these peoples' ethnical development and was a brake preventing their drawing closer to Tadjik supporters of Sunnism. The interference of the Afghan fundamentalists in the civil war in Tadjikistan (1992 - 1994) greatly accentuated the importance of the Pamiran peoples living on both sides of the Tadjik-Afghan border. The fact that both Tadjik and Afghan Muslim fundamentalists managed to find refuge and support amongst the people of Gorniy Badakhshan is indicative of the important role played by Sunnite and Shiite fundamentalism in this region.

Relations with the Authorities

Relations with the authorities became a serious problem for the Muslim clergy only with the annexation of Central Asia to Russia in 1864 - 1885; this put Central Asian Muslims under the rule of a non-Muslim secular state for the first time in many centuries. The loss of the almost limitless power which had been enjoyed by the theocratic khanates and the enforced subordination to the

Russian administration was taken very badly by all categories of the Central Asian clergy. It is no coincidence that it was the latter that became Russia's main and most consistent opponent in Central Asia, notwithstanding the extremely cautious policy adopted by the Russian administration with regard to Islam and Islamic institutions. It should be noted, however, that in the period between Russia's conquest of Central Asia and the establishment of Soviet rule the position of the Muslim clergy in different parts of the region was by no means identical. Whereas the Khokand khanate suffered liquidation - its entire territory being absorbed by the new General-Governorship of Turkestan - the emirate of Bukhara and the Khivan khanate, although subject to large territorial losses, nevertheless managed to retain a degree of independence; under the terms of an agreement signed in 1873 they were placed under the protectorate of Russia. The Russian political agent Lessar, taking the example of Bukhara, described Russian policy in these khanates in the following terms: 'The system we adopt with respect to a khanate is based upon complete non-interference in its internal affairs. Our concern is for the stability of the Bukhara market, as well as for political and strategic goals ... the emir and his officials can do with their people whatever they want. In this way, without expenditure of resources or effort, we get from Bukhara all that we need'[51]. Russia's refusal to admit Bukhara into the Russian Empire is to be explained not so much by the desire not to strain relations with England or by a reluctance to take upon itself unwanted expenditure, as by an attempt to use Bukhara's religious authority to strengthen Russian influence in neighbouring Muslim countries. Thus the Muslim clergy of Bukhara and Khiva managed on the whole to retain its privileges and influences in those Russian protectorates - although, of course, this influence and these privileges were now by no means unlimited. At the same time, Russia intervened in the religious affairs of the Central Asian khanates only in exceptional circumstances. Following the pogroms against the Shiites in 1910, for example, those responsible for the troubles were dismissed from their posts and exiled from Bukhara at the request of the Russian political agent. The Muslim clergy in what had been the Khokand khanate found themselves in an altogether different position, being under the constant and direct control of the Russian administration of Turkestan. Not surprisingly, it was here, in the Fergana Valley in the 1880s and 1890s, that the Russians met with the greatest resistance from the Muslim clergy. The latter were generally headed by ishans, i.e. by the unofficial section of the local clergy. Many ishans declared themselves the legitimate khans of Khokand and called upon the Muslim faithful to take up arms against 'the infidels'. About 50 such 'khans' were captured. The phenomenon became known as the movement of the dzhetim-khans ('false khans'). All these incidents were purely local in character and easily suppressed by the Russian administration. Rather more serious were the troubles of 1885 organized by the Dervish-khan, a large landowner and former official of the khanate. He similarly proclaimed himself khan of Khokand, but acted in collaboration with the ishans of Fergana. The largest anti-Russian action organized by the ishans, though, was the Andizhan uprising of 1898. This was led by the ishan of the Naqshbandi order, Muhammad-Ali (Madali), who, having enlisted the support of the Sultan of Turkey, declared jihad against the Russians, but was quickly defeated in a clash with regular Russian forces. With the aim of undermining the economic prospects of Russia's opponents in Central Asia (namely, the Muslim clergy and feudal aristocracy), in 1886 Kaufman, the first Governor-General of Turkestan, initiated a series of radical agrarian reforms. The essence of this openly 'Bolshevik' initiative was that land was to be made the property of those who cultivated it. In this way the local feudal aristocracy and clergy were stripped of 90% of the land they had originally owned[52]. This reform did not lead to any increase of warm sentiment towards the Russians, but did significantly weaken the economic influence of Russia's opponents. The Russian protectorates of the emirate of Bukhara and the Khivan khanate were not affected by the new measures.

The Andizhan uprising of 1898 put the Russian administration on its guard against the Muslim clergy. As a result, there was an increase in Russian control over religious teaching establishments and over contacts between the Central Asian clergy and Turkey. However, right up to the beginning of the First World War, Central Asia's Muslim clergy preferred to avoid direct confrontation with the Turkestan administration. The Young Turk revolution of 1908 - 1909; the coming to power in Turkey of the pan-Turkic party 'Unity and progress'; the increase of activity at this time amongst the local jadids - all this helped to move the main area of conflict from the religious and Islamic sphere to the national or pan-Turkic one. The greatest source of anxiety for the authorities at the time was the activities of Turkish emissaries. 'Here,' wrote the Turkestan Governor-General to the Minister of War in March 1909, 'there are fanatical preachers of Islam appearing from Arabia ... agents of the Young Turks'. In 1910 the Governor-General of Turkestan announced that merely 'in the first half of this year twice as many preachers of Islam have entered the country as in the whole of 1909'[53].

The First World War complicated relations between the Russian administration and the Central Asian clergy still more. Turkey's participation in the war as an opponent of Russia and the defeats suffered by the Russian troops on the German front made the Central Asian Muslim clergy excessively bold. As always, the first to come forward with anti-Russian incitements were the ishans - but on this occasion not merely the ishans of Turkestan, but those of Bukhara and Khiva as well. In February 1915 the famous Bukharan ishan Shayakhsi called upon Muslims to take part in a general uprising against the Russians. Propaganda spread by the ishans played a not insignificant role in the organization of the largest anti-Russian revolt in Central Asia in 1916, in the course of which ishans such as Nazyr-Hadji declared ghazawat, or holy war, against Russia. The official Muslim clergy in Tashkent, however, refused to join the revolt (although it did not conceal its sympathy for the rebels). A similar position was taken by the Muslim leaders in Bukhara and Khiva.

The February and October revolutions of 1917, which led to the civil war of 1918 - 1921, created a short-lived political vacuum in Central Asia. This the local Muslim clergy lost no time in exploiting in order to strengthen their position. The imposition of Soviet rule initially in Turkestan, and then in Bukhara and Khiva, marked the beginning of an entirely new stage in relations between authorities and clergy. From this time forwards all categories of clergy in all regions of Central Asia were under the rigid control of the totalitarian Soviet system. The liberalism and tolerance of the old Russian administration was now something that could only be dreamed about. In practice the Marxist-Leninist ideology meant not merely the separation of religion and state and the secularization of all areas of life, but also the public opening of hostilities against Islam, which was now considered an ideological enemy. In this lay the essential difference between the militant atheism of the Communists in Central Asia and the policy of laicism (secularism) followed by the Kemalists in Turkey. At the same time, however, it should be noted that in the initial period of Communist rule (1918 - 1928, approximately) the Communist attitude to Islam was extremely cautious. This is to be explained by the following factors:

1. an understanding of the role played by Islam in the lives of the peoples of Central Asia;

2. the rather special attitude to Islam taken by the Communist Party of Turkestan, and the considerable influence held by local Muslim Communists;

3. attempts to export the revolution into neighbouring Muslim countries;

4. the Basmach movement in Central Asia.

The second period in relations between Communism and Islam began at the end of the 1920s and lasted until Germany's attack on the USSR in June 1941. This period was characterized by total secularization of the entire region and by severe suppression of the activities of the Central Asian clergy. Those who suffered most were ishans well-known for anti-Russian agitations in the past. The abrupt hardening of Communist policy was caused both by the consolidation of the Soviet regime in the USSR and by the strengthening of the positions of Stalin and his group in the Party and state apparat. In Central Asia itself, the Basmach movement was almost entirely liquidated (with the exception of regions in South Tadjikistan), and the local communist parties were 'purged' of Muslims. The attempt to export the revolution to neighbouring countries in the Muslim East was put off until another, better time. At the November plenary session of the Communist Party in 1929 Stalin announced an all-out attack against class enemies in the cities and in the country, whilst proclaiming a new historical stage in the building of communism[54]. Industrialization went ahead in the cities of Central Asia; country settlements were plunged into intensive collectivization. The Muslim clergy were viewed by the Communists as a typical class enemy. Some were accordingly repressed; others fled abroad; those who remained were forced to become a submissive instrument in the hands of the Soviet authorities. The position of the Muslim clergy deteriorated still further when, in the middle of the 1930s, Stalin put forward his new conception of intensified class struggle as a means of advancing towards socialism; this conception was to become the theoretical basis for the mass repressions of 1937. The very fact that by the beginning of the 1940s there were 20 times fewer mosques than there had been before the Revolution (in spite of an increase in the size of the Muslim population) is indication of the extreme persecution which Islam was under (as were all religions in the USSR)[55]. Only the arrival of the Second World War put a stop to the Soviet authorities' merciless attack on Central Asian Islam. During the war, needing the support of the local population as well as the positive neutrality of neighbouring Muslim countries, the Communist Party relaxed its 'class' policies towards Islam and improved the position of the Muslim clergy. Following the war, the need to restore the shattered economy and the ideological de-stalinization of the time were factors in prolonging the relative lull in relations between the authorities and Islam; this lull lasted until the beginning of the 1960s. The first half of the 1960s, however, were marked by new attacks from the authorities - attacks which were provoked by the 22nd Congress of the Communist Party and its adoption of a programme for building communism. The new ideological principles ruled out peaceful co-existence with any religion, and let alone with a religion so 'backward and reactionary' as Islam. Islam was accused of barbarity, primitivism, anti-modernism, anti-feminism, and of being an impediment to friendship between nations. This period, though, did not last long - until the middle of the 1960s. Nikita Khruschev's removal from power in 1964 and the appearance of new Muslim allies of the USSR in the Third World, and in particular in the Arab East, caused relations with Islam to take another sharp turn. Out of a desire to make socialism more attractive for the Muslim nations, the Soviet authorities put a halt to open attacks on Islam and the Muslim clergy, and began to propagandize a new conception according to which Islam could serve progressive goals just as well as reactionary ones. It goes without saying that the right to evaluate the role played by Islam in various countries was assigned by the Soviet ideologues to themselves. The progressiveness of the Muslim clergy was to be judged on the basis of the latter's political views and attitude to socialism and the USSR. In practice, this conception proved very convenient and was used widely both in home and foreign policy-making until the disintegration of the Soviet Union in 1991. The reforms initiated by Mikhail Gorbachev during the period of 'glasnost' and 'perestroika' put an end to atheistic propaganda and, for the first time in all the years of Soviet rule, gave the Muslim clergy a measure of freedom of action. The subsequent declaration of independence by the Central Asian republics and the latter's solemn announcement of their Muslim character signalled liberation for Central Asian Islam, but not, however, for the official clergy, which remained under the control of the ex-communist leadership (control which was, though, not as humiliating or severe as previously). The situation of the unofficial Muslim clergy is more complicated. The latter had always been harder for the authorities to control, and were considerably closer than the official clergy to the common people. Today, as in the past, the ishans and those with a claim to the role of the ishans oppose both the authorities and the official clergy; many have adopted positions which are openly fundamentalist. Their extremism is to be explained not so much by the influence of Iranian and Afghan fundamentalists as by the persecution to which Islam was subject over the course of many years, and by the fact that the official clergy was forcibly controlled by the authorities. Only pressure from the Soviet authorities can explain statements made by the former Head of the Muslim Spiritual Board of Central Asia and Kazakhstan, mufti Ziyautdinkhan ibn Ishan Babakhan. He, for example, asserted that 'if a non-Muslim state, whilst guaranteeing Muslims the opportunity to follow the instructions of their religion - as does the Soviet Union, - at the same time helps them to attain modern civilization and free themselves from a condition of political dependence and economic backwardness, that state is indeed doing much to fulfil the aims set by Islam'[56]. Another member of the official Muslim clergy, the imam-khatyb of the principal mosque of Talkhatan-Baba (in the Iolotan region of Turkmenistan), went still further during discussion of the draft of the last Soviet constitution. At a crowded meeting of Muslims he declared that 'a very large number of articles in the draft constitution are close to the teaching of the sacred Koran and the utterances of the prophet Muhammad. We wholly and entirely approve this draft'[57]. The Soviet authorities demanded support from the higher clergy not only in internal, but in foreign affairs as well. In an interview with Soviet journalists on the 11th January 1980 the above-mentioned Sheikh Babakhan declared that 'today, when imperialists and reactionaries are trying impudently to interfere in the internal affairs of the Democratic Republic of Afghanistan, Soviet Muslims again want to make clear their brotherly solidarity with the freedom-loving people of Afghanistan and wish the Afghan people much success in converting their ancient country into a modern, independent and prosperous state'[58]. The loyalty of the official Muslim clergy to the Soviet authorities was noticed also by eminent specialists on Islam in the USSR such as A. Bennigsen and C. Lemercier-Quelquejay, who emphasized that not only had no mullah ever challenged the Soviet state, but there had never been any sign of opposition to the regime from the official clergy[59]. Notwithstanding the pronounced dependence of the official Muslim clergy on the Soviet regime, it would be wrong to attribute the clergy's loyalty merely to pressure from the authorities. The enormous advances in economic, social and cultural development amongst the Muslim nations of Central Asia, combined with a standard of living which is higher than in neighbouring Islamic countries, could not fail to exert an influence on the region's Muslim clergy. The majority of specialists in the West consider the above to be one of the indisputable merits of the Soviet system[60].

Following the declaration of independence by the Central Asian states, the official clergy became an ally of the authorities in the conflict with the Muslim fundamentalists. Almost all the representatives of the official clergy have declared themselves opposed to the formation of a party on a religious basis. 'That should not be allowed to happen,' declared, for instance, the mufti of Kazakhstan, Ratbek Nysanbaev. 'We should not forget, when it comes down to it, that religion is an eternal law whereas a party is simply a policy, which is subject to change; it is a sin when politicians want to use Islam for the fulfilment of their own narrowly ambitious goals'[61]. At the same time attempts to break away from under the control of the authorities are usually unsuccessful. In Uzbekistan, for instance, when mufti Muhammad Sadyk Yusuf, the Head of the Muslim Spiritual Board for Central Asia indulged in criticism of the president Islam Karimov, he was dismissed from the post he held as spiritual head of the Muslims. The mufti was accused of financial misconduct, and his office was searched.

In general, the position of the official clergy following the disintegration of the USSR has become noticeably more difficult. Previously, the official clergy had to reckon only with the authorities; now it has to act whilst keeping an eye open for both the Islamic fundamentalists and the local nationalists. Moreover, as yet its relations with neither group are on a firm footing. The Muslim fundamentalists and the nationalists accuse the official clergy of betraying the ideals of Islam and of complicity with the authorities. Sometimes the verbal warfare between the two parties crosses over into open clashes. At the end of 1991, for instance Kazakh nationalists seized the residence of the mufti of Kazakhstan, beat up the mufti, and declared that he had been dismissed from his post. Only the intervention of the authorities and the arrest of his attackers saved the mufti from violent reprisals. The events of 1992 - 1995 show that in almost all the Central Asian republics (with the exception of Tadjikistan) the ex-communist leadership has more or less succeeded in retaining control - even if of a noticeably weaker variety - over the official clergy. On the other hand, the official clergy itself, having lost some part of its influence over the common people as a result of the opposition it faces from the nationalists and Muslim fundamentalists, is in need of the support of the authorities. This explains why the Central Asian leaders, for as long as they maintain a firm hold on the political and economic situation in their countries, will be ensured the loyalty of the official clergy. At the present time the chief problem confronting both the authorities and the official clergy is not their mutual relations with each other, but their opposition to Muslim fundamentalism. In the fight with the latter, the ruling regimes cannot get by without the official clergy, whilst the official clergy are unable to face the extremists without help from the authorities. On the other hand, open collaboration with the present authorities involves the risk of sharing the latter's fate in a post-communist Central Asia where the prevailing atmosphere is one of political uncertainty.

The Muslim Renaissance and its Opponents

The revival of Islam in Central Asia began at the end of the 1980s when Mikhail Gorbachev's policy of 'perestroika' and 'glasnost' allowed people in the USSR, for the first time in all the years of Soviet rule, a measure of religious freedom. The revival of Muslim religious life saw the immediate emergence of two different directions. The first direction was under the control of both the authorities and the official clergy; its visible result was a sharp increase in the number and level of activity of Muslim institutions. In 1990 - 1991, for example, the number of working mosques alone increased from 160 to 5000. The building of new mosques and madrasahs was financed by Arab countries, and Iran and Turkey, who were competing for influence amongst the Central Asian Muslims; such operations were carried out legally, for the most part, and without opposition from the authorities. The second - and far more radical - direction in the Muslim renaissance was shaped by the unofficial Muslim clergy. The latter had been subject to the most intense persecution during the years of Soviet rule, and this had had an evident effect on the radicality of their views. From the very beginning, and especially in Tadjikistan and in the Uzbek part of the Fergana Valley, the unofficial clergy took up fundamentalist positions and were hostile to both the ex-communist leadership and the official clergy, whom they accused of collaboration with the authorities. The fundamentalists immediately began to set up, alongside legal institutions, a complex network of underground cells; these cells allowed them very quickly to escape the control of the authorities. Because of the existence of this parallel and highly secret network of organizations, subsequent bans on the Islamists' activities proved ineffective.

Officially, the first legal Islamic party was founded a year before the break-up of the Soviet Union, in the summer of 1990, in the city of Astrakhan (Russia). As was the case before the October Revolution (1917), the initiators of the new Islamic party were Tatar Muslim activists. The choice of location for the party was also not accidental: Astrakhan, the capital of the Tatar khanate, was annexed to Russia in the middle of the 16th century. The founding congress, attended by representatives from the majority of the Muslim nations of the USSR, announced the formation of the Party of Islamic Renaissance. For political reasons (the Communists were still in power), the compilers of the party's programme limited themselves to a document of great modesty which emphasized that the party's activities were aimed at providing Muslims with the opportunity to live according to the demands of their religion. The unofficial pronouncements of the party's leaders, however, left no doubt that their goal was in fact the creation of an Islamic state, and that they themselves were Muslim fundamentalists. On returning to Central Asia from the congress in Astrakhan, the members of the new party made attempts to set up regional branches of the party in their own republics, but did not succeed in doing so through legal means. This was not simply because the communist leadership of the Central Asian republics was significantly less democratic than its Russian counterpart. The local authorities understood very well that a liberal attitude towards Islamism, though possible in Russia, could have very dangerous consequences in Muslim Central Asia. For this reason in almost all the Central Asian republics (with the exception of Tadjikistan) the activists of the Party of Islamic

Renaissance were forced to conduct their constituent assemblies underground. In Tadjikistan, as everywhere else in Central Asia, their application for registration of a new party also initially met with refusal. However, as it transpired, the position of the Muslim fundamentalists was considerably stronger, and the influence of the communist leadership considerably weaker, in this republic than in other Central Asian republics. The unofficial clergy was traditionally very influential here, and this played a decisive role in strengthening the position of the extremists. In October 1990 activists of the Party of Islamic Renaissance managed to hold a constituent assembly of the Tadjik branch of the party almost without hindrance, under the eyes of the authorities. Subsequently, it was the Tadjik fundamentalists who were able to exploit best of all the state of shock which overcame the communist leadership following the failure of the coup attempt in August 1991. Their influence grew quickly. In October 1991 the official ban on the activities of the Party of Islamic Renaissance in Tadjikistan was revoked, and the party held its first legal congress, attended by 657 delegates representing 20 000 party members[62]. In the struggle against the Communists the Tadjik fundamentalists succeeded, as subsequent events were to show, in obtaining the support of both the nationalists and the democrats. Moreover in Tadjikistan, unlike in the other Central Asian republics, the Muslim fundamentalists became the main oppositional force, acting as an organizing focus for weaker anti-Communist groups of a nationalist or democratic character. Attempts by the ex-communist leadership to play along with Islam and find points of compromise agreeable to both sides led to nothing - or rather, as a result of concessions made, only strengthened the hand of the Islamists. As a result, the ex-communists, stripped of ideological and political legitimacy in the eyes of the population, tried to avoid using force and quickly lost control of the situation. In September and October 1992, after receiving a large quantity of armaments from the Afghan mujahidin, the Tadjik Islamists decided openly to seize power. The ex-communists, headed by President Rakhmon Nabiev, turned to Russia with a request for help, but were refused. On the 25th October 1992 the Islamists, supported by groups of nationalists and democrats, succeeded, after intense fighting, in seizing the capital of the republic, Dushanbe. Nabiev was forced to retire, but his supporters, unwilling to accept his retirement, continued to fight. The civil war in Tadjikistan added new fuel to the old enmity between the north and south of the republic, and brought the interests of the various clans into collision with each other. The northerners, who are distinguishable even by the way they look (having a lighter shade of skin), have always considered themselves superior and, in the past - including during Soviet times - filled the majority of administrative posts. Nabiev, for example, was born in the northern town of Khodzhent (formerly Leninabad). The coalition between the Islamists, nationalists and democrats was, in the main, a coalition of southerners. During the years of Soviet rule the south of Tadjikistan, including the region of Dushanbe, developed at a faster pace than the north, and this led to a breach of the historical equilibrium between the various regions. The southerners demanded greater representation in the organs of power. The regional and clan conflict was most vividly exemplified in the presidential elections in Tadjikistan in November 1991. The north's candidate was Rakhmon Nabiev, head of the Communist Party of Tadjikistan until 1985; the south was represented by Davlat Khudnazarov, a famous director and a man without either party or religious affiliation who had the support of the Islamists, nationalists and democrats from the south of the country. Thus the fight against the Communists was in fact based on a regional rivalry between north and south. The elections were won by the ex-communists from the north: Nabiev received 57% of the votes; Khudnazarov, 31%. The subsequent short-lived revenge of the southern Islamists can hardly be considered a victory for Muslim fundamentalism. Rather, it would be more correct to talk of exploitation of the factor of regional rivalry by the Tadjik Islamists. The latter, however, failed to take account of one very important circumstance: the possibility of a reaction from the ex-communist leaders of other Central Asian republics, and especially of neighbouring Uzbekistan. The victory of the Islamists in Dushanbe delivered a severe fright to Islam Karimov, the Uzbek President, who very rightly feared a domino effect, whereby the fall of secular power in Tadjikistan would bring crashing down post-communist regimes all over Central Asia. An additional concern was that at least 20% of the population of Tadjikistan consisted of Uzbeks. This explains Islam Karimov's decision to send his crack troops to help the northern ex-communists. In this he had the support of the leaders of the other Central Asian republics as well as the tacit assent of Moscow. In December 1992 Uzbek tanks bearing Tadjik flags took Dushanbe by storm, whilst Uzbek aeroplanes bombed the Islamist bases in the Pamir mountains and Uzbek security forces guarded the new Tadjik government (which was headed by the President of the Supreme Soviet of Tadjikistan, Imamaly Rakhmonov). The Tadjik Islamists and the Afghan mujahidin who supported them were driven from their positions almost everywhere, even in the regions of Kulyab and Kurgan-Tube, where the Islamist opposition had strongholds. Use of the Uzbek army would have been impossible without the assent of the Russian military command, which to this day secretly controls, supplies and trains the armed forces of all the Central Asian states. Russian politicians and military had good reason to fear that the idea of militant fundamentalism would spread throughout Central Asia and head westward from the Urals into Tatarstan, then engaged in a fight for its independence. The option of intervening in events in Tadjikistan was, however, rejected by the new Russian leadership, which had no desire to link itself with the corrupt Communist circles of 'the time of stagnation'. According to the views held by Boris Yeltsin and his team, it was best for democratic Russia to rid itself of the problems caused by its Muslim republics with all possible haste. Moreover, memories of the unsuccessful war against the Muslim fundamentalists in Afghanistan were still painfully fresh. Thus, following consultation with the leaders of the Central Asian republics, a decision was taken to send the Uzbek army into Tadjikistan. The Russian troops in Tadjikistan were given the task of guarding the Russian population, which continued to be responsible for keeping the entire economy of the republic running. For the attempt to establish Islamist fundamentalist rule in Tadjikistan the population of this small republic paid very dearly: there were more than 20 000 deaths; 120 000 Tadjiks fled to Afghanistan; and about half a million people were left homeless. As a result of the war, the Tadjik economy was reduced to a state of complete collapse, and will require many years before it can be restored. Furthermore, the return of the ex-communists to power has not stopped the bloodshed in Tadjikistan. Instead of putting down arms after the military defeat they had suffered, the Tadjik fundamentalists retreated to Afghanistan, where they received large-scale support from the Islamic Party of Afghanistan headed by Hekmatyar. Helped by the local population, they mount periodic attacks on the Russian border posts and carry out partisan raids deep into Tadjik territory. Like the Afghan mujahidin, the Tadjik fundamentalists call themselves 'irreconcilable' and have declared that they will continue to fight even if 'the pro-Communist and pro-Russian government gains control over the entire territory of the republic'[63]. A declaration of this kind can be regarded only as an intention to continue the war from Afghan territory.

Following its painful experience in Tadjikistan, the Party of Islamic Renaissance closed down its regional branches in all the Central Asian republics. The Islamic fundamentalists went underground. After Tadjikistan, their influence is strongest in Uzbekistan, particularly in the Fergana Valley. In 1991 - 1992, for example, Namangan, the largest city in the Fergana Valley, was almost paralyzed by a division of power: whilst the authorities had control of the city's new districts, the older part of the city was ruled by the Islamic fundamentalists; here traditional Muslim law was in force. According to unofficial information, the Uzbek Islamists succeeded in holding their constituent assembly underground, and in 1993 the Uzbek branch of the Party of Islamic Renaissance numbered around 10 000 members. Uzbek fundamentalist leaders addressed an appeal to the republic's leadership in which they asserted that 'Uzbekistan should be an Islamic state. The Uzbek people has no sympathy for, and no understanding of, Western values, and any politician who takes it into his head to impose these values on the nation's consciousness will be making a big mistake' . The appeal went on to recommend that 'we should follow the example of the Islamic republic of Iran, which has rid itself of the false ideals of the West and gone its own way, paving the way for all other countries in the region'[64]. In reply to numerous such appeals from the fundamentalists, Islam Karimov has limited himself to the cautious statement that 'the fundamentalists can profess whatever opinions they have, but they should not call for changes in the constitutional structure of the republic'[65]. The growing influence of militant Islamic fundamentalism, however, combined with the tragic events in Tadjikistan, have forced the ex-communist leadership of Uzbekistan to give up experiments with democracy and turn to a strict authoritarian policy with regard to all opposition to their regime. The 'Islamic spring' which set in in 1990 had by the beginning of 1992 given way to harsh winter. The Islamic Party of Uzbekistan (never registered), the 'Adolat' ('Fairness') movement and other religious organizations were crushed; the leaders of the 'Islamic spring' were put on trial and sentenced to various terms of imprisonment[66]. Muslim fundamentalists were not alone in being persecuted; the same treatment was given to members of the democratic and nationalist organizations. These measures, however, have failed to eliminate the threat of destabilization posed by Islamic fundamentalism. Reports by the national security forces paint a threatening picture. Tadjikistan continues to act as a channel through which arms, extremist religious literature, fighters and fundamentalists propagandists flow into Uzbekistan. Tourist, business and even diplomatic channels are widely used for the same purpose. In 1993 alone, more than 50 Islamic emissaries were caught and thrown out of Uzbekistan; several batches of armaments were intercepted; and, not far from Fergana, stores of military supplies were unearthed, together with camps for fighters undergoing special training for an anticipated Islamic coup[67]. In 1993 - 1994, in connection with the growth of the Islamic fundamentalist threat, strict control was placed over the content of sermons in the mosques, and over sources of financial support for priests and religious institutions. All deviations by religious activists from the prescribed rules now end in dismissal or even arrest. Religious activists are forbidden to express their views in the media, to leave the country without special permission, to associate with colleagues from other countries, and so on. Believers now have difficulty in building mosques even on their own money. The Uzbek authorities have tightened up the system by which visas are granted, exercise careful control over all bank, commercial and charitable operations involving companies from Muslim countries, and have closed down all banks suspected of links with Islamic fundamentalist organizations. President Karimov considers his greatest achievement to be peace and stability in Uzbekistan. 'We are ready to knock sense into hundreds of troublemakers ,' he warned, 'if the stability of the republic calls for it'[68]. In the opinion of a majority of political observers, Uzbekistan, with its powerful economy and the largest population in Central Asia, is the key to the whole region. The numerous Uzbek minorities in neighbouring Central Asian republics give Uzbekistan added political pull. Thus, victory for the Islamic fundamentalists in Uzbekistan would mean their accession to power throughout Central Asia - and vice-versa. This explains why the openly secularist policy pursued by the ex-communist leadership of Uzbekistan ensures it the support both of the West and of Russia, drowning out the latter countries' criticism of human rights violations in the republic.

The increasing influence of Islam in post-Soviet Central Asia forces all political forces in the region - and not merely the ex-communists - to make serious allowance for this factor in their policy-making. It is worth noting that even the former President of Kyrgyzstan, Askar Akaev - a democrat dependent on an alliance with the ex-communists, - was forced to assure his parliament that 'Kyrgyzstan will be a Muslim state in which Islamic values will prevail over universal human ones'[69]. All the Central Asian republics have officially declared themselves Muslim states, and President Karimov of Uzbekistan , well-known for his uncompromising struggle against Muslim fundamentalism, even found himself having to go down on his knees during an election campaign as a sign of respect towards Islam.

Outlook

The Muslim Renaissance in Central Asia has to be perceived as a natural and inevitable phenomenon following the 70 years of Soviet rule. As was only to be expected, attempts to ban Islam, to use it to export revolution or for the purpose of building socialism, have been unsuccessful. The majority of the native population of Central Asia has retained its Muslim faith. Islam represents an integral system of conduct in life which it was beyond the power of the Soviet regime to destroy. It would be more correct to say that the Soviet system came to accept the existence of Islam, whilst Islam adapted itself to suit the dogmas of the Marxist-Leninist ideology.

The break-up of the USSR in 1991 to a large extent returned Central Asia to the situation it was in before the imposition of Soviet rule. However, just as it is impossible to enter the same river twice, so it is impossible to make any direct comparison between Central Asia in post-communist and pre-Soviet times. The long years of Soviet rule have left a heavy imprint on Central Asian Islam. Muslim religious institutions have suffered worst of all: the number of mosques and madrasahs has decreased by tens, and in some districts by hundreds, of times. A severe blow was delivered to the unofficial Muslim clergy - to the ishans, who were notable for their lack of submissiveness to the authorities even in pre-Soviet times. The majority of ishans have shared the fate of members of the Basmach movement. The official clergy had a much easier time. The Soviet regime aimed not to eliminate the official clergy, but to tame it, and in this was largely successful. The sudden increase in Muslim extremism was a direct result of the violence inflicted over many years on the living soul of Islam. This increase was caused not so much by external influences - Iranian policy-making or the military aid coming from Afghanistan - as by a reaction amongst Central Asian Muslims to the militant atheism of the local and Russian communists. The second most important factor was the dramatic weakening of the position of the official Muslim clergy during the years of Soviet rule. All this has led to a situation untypical of the history of Central Asian Islam: the Turkic Sunnite nations, well-known for the moderation of their religious views, have unexpectedly proved a source of large-scale support for the Islamic fundamentalists. On the other hand, there is good reason to suppose that this is only a temporary phenomenon, and that a cautious, controlled de-Sovietization of Central Asia will reduce the influence of the fundamentalists - at least in those regions where the Turkic peoples are in the majority. A lot will depend on an improvement in the position of the official clergy, which has almost always exerted a moderating influence on the faithful in times of crisis. Events in Tadjikistan and in the city of Namangan in Uzbekistan have shown the authorities how important is the development of mutual relations with the unofficial clergy, which tends to have more radical views. In the final analysis, the ability of the ex-communist leadership to preserve economic and political stability in the Central Asian states, even if this is effected by authoritarian means, will have a decisive importance for the future of Islam in Central Asia.

Chapter Four

THE COTTON EPIC

Although cotton has been cultivated in Central Asia for more than two thousand years, it began to play an important role in the Central Asian economy only after the region became part of Russia. In spite of its great size, the Russian Empire contained no region climatically suitable for the cultivation of the cotton plant. Such quantities of cotton as were needed by Russian industry were imported from abroad, mainly from the USA - a situation which was considered tolerable whilst Russia remained an agrarian country and experienced no difficulty in importing cotton for its relatively small textile industry. The situation changed dramatically, though, when, on the one hand, Russia underwent a rapid industrial revolution following the abolition of serfdom in 1861, and, on the other, import of cotton from the USA ceased as a result of the civil war of 1861 - 1865. The need of Russia's rapidly-developing industry for cotton was a factor in the Russian government's decision to conquer Central Asia in 1864 - 85.

The Economic Policy of the Tsarist Regime in Turkestan

In consideration of natural and climatic, economic and demographic factors, the Russian government divided Central Asia into two parts: northern and southern. The north and north-east (Kazakhstan and Kyrgyzstan), regions where for reasons of climate cotton cultivation was impossible, and where small populations lived a nomadic life, were viewed as a reserve of land for peasants migrating from European Russia and Eastern Ukraine. The southern regions (Uzbekistan, Tadjikistan and Turkmenistan), where a large and settled population was concentrated in a few oases climatically favourable for the production of cotton, it was proposed to use as the basis of Russian cotton production. This functional division of Central Asia suited the interests of both industrial capital with its need for home-produced cotton, and of the large Russian landowners, for whom it was important that the landless peasantry should be resettled. Subsequently the Russian government took the following steps to stimulate the development of cotton cultivation in Central Asia:

1. It switched to an openly protectionist policy, significantly increasing the taxes raised on cotton imported from abroad. If imported cotton was taxed at 40 kopecks per pood (1 pood = 16kg) in 1878, in 1894 this tax had already risen to 3 rubles and 15 kopecks per pood[70].

2. It took active steps to introduce better-quality, American varieties of cotton plant. The native Central Asian plant had a very short fibre and was inclined to be very dirty[71]. If in 1884 only 300 dessiatini (1 dessiatina = 1.09 hectares) of land

were sown with American varieties of cotton plant, by 1890 58,850 dessiatin were sown with these varieties[72].

3.   It established tax privileges on land planted with American varieties of cotton plant. Land planted with American cotton was taxed at the same rate as land planted with wheat and other crops. But since the income from a dessiatina planted with cotton was 4 - 5 times higher than from a desiatina planted with other crops, the peasants began to show a preference for American cotton as their chosen crop. The supplantation of the native Central Asian cotton plant (guza) proceeded with extraordinary rapidity; by the beginning of the 20th century in the main agricultural regions of Turkestan the native plant had been entirely replaced by American varieties. The guza plant survived slightly longer in Bukhara, where cotton production was less-developed due to preservation of a residual independence from Russia.

Russian policy in Turkestan was laid out with absolute clarity by Krivoschein, the Minister for Agriculture, after his trip to Turkestan in 1912: ' ... The present development of cotton plantations,' he wrote, 'can and should be intensified still further by means of further reduction in the quantity of grain crops planted on irrigated land ... Every extra pood of Turkestan wheat means extra competition for Siberian and Kuban wheat; every pood of Turkmestan cotton means competition for American cotton. Therefore it is better to give the territory imported wheat - even at extra cost - but to make irrigated land available for cotton-growing'[73]. As a result of the colossal expansion of cotton-planting at the beginning of the 20th century Turkestan began to experience a deficit of wheat; from this time forwards wheat was systematically imported from Russia, which strengthened still further Central

Asia's economic dependence on the metropolis. Initially, follow-ing the example of the USA, the Russian administration specifi-cally encouraged cotton-growing on large plantations. A Russian economist of the time gave the following description of the cotton fever: 'The 1880s and 90s - the dawn of the rising cotton sun - were a time of Americanism in the Russian cotton-producing business. Hundreds of officials, officers and other state employees and mer-chants threw themselves into the growing of cotton. Tashkent and its neighbouring districts were particularly affected by the passion for cotton-cultivation. Ghostly visions of golden rain, the dream of American wealth in Turkestan, eclipsed everything else'[74]. But the era of large plantations did not last long. Plantation owners very quickly went bankrupt. Subsequently it emerged that the most profitable way to cultivate cotton in Central Asian conditions was on peasant smallholdings. The failure of the cotton plantations was related to a certain extent to the radical agrarian reform con-ducted by Russia in Turkestan (Khiva and Bukhara were spared this reform, as they were only under a Russian protectorate). In an endeavour to weaken the positions of the anti-Russian-minded feudal landed aristocracy and Islamic priesthood, the Tsar's ad-ministration in Turkestan put into practice a slogan later to be employed by the Bolsheviks, 'Land to those who work it', making the peasants owners of all the land which they had previously used to rent from native landlords and religious institutions. The nu-merous and - for the peasants - unaffordable taxes in operation at the time were replaced by a single government land tax at a rate of 10%. The main result of this reform was the liquidation of the feudal landowning class in Turkestan and a significant improve-ment in the standard of living of the peasants, who became small-scale landowners. These revolutionary measures had a further consequence: a deficit of cheap labour for the cotton plantations (cotton is a highly labour-intensive plant), and the resulting trans-formation of the peasant small-holding into the main supplier of cotton. For the small-holding - and in Turkestan smallholdings made up almost 80% of agricultural establishments - there was only one way to survive, and this was to sow cotton: at the prices and in the conditions of land shortage prevailing at the time no other agricultural crop was capable of feeding the peasant fam-ily and of providing work for all its members. The main district for cotton cultivation was the Fergana Valley, famous for its fertile lands and favourable climate. In folk art the invasion of cotton into Central Asia was depicted in highly tragic colours. According to a Russian contemporary of the beginning of the cotton epic, the district of Fergana was in the 1880s inundated with predictions that 'the white fluff would bring black calamity to people' ; the same source tells us that the Islamic priesthood led an active and intense campaign against cotton. A large number of the Fergana peasantry believed in the superstition that 'Allah will allow only so much fluff as is needed to make for each member of the family three smocks a year'[75].

Cotton as the Stimulus for Economic Growth

The intensive cultivation of cotton led to two developments which were new to Central Asia: 1) the construction of railways; and 2) the development of industry. Before it became part of the Russian Empire, Central Asia had not a single industrial en-terprise or railway. And although the first railway (Krasnovodsk - Ashkhabad - Merv, Turkmenistan) was built for strategic military reasons, subsequent development of the railway network was mo-tivated above all by the need to transport cotton out of Central

Asia to the metropolis. The same motivation dictated the appearance of the cotton-refining and oil-producing industries, for transportation of unprocessed cotton to Central Russia was unprofitable. The first industrial centres were set up in areas of cotton cultivation in the Fergana Valley, and were owned, in the main, by Russian entrepreneurs, since native capital was active only in trade and agriculture, and even in the latter fields was mainly involved in money-lending.

Cotton brought into Central Asia not merely industry and railways, but an influx of Russians as well. If the majority of the unskilled labour force were made up of the local population - Uzbeks in the main, - almost all the qualified workers, on the other hand, were Russian. Still more Russians were employed in the construction and servicing of the railways, whilst the first purely Russian cities arose on the sites of railway stations. In 1899 a finish was put to the so-called 'Central Asian' railway, which stretched over a distance of more than 2000 km, and joined the regions where cotton was produced to those in which it was consumed. When Central Asian cotton began to be exported along this line, the caravan roads - which had operated right up to this moment - immediately lost their importance.

With the introduction of American cotton the Turkestan peasantry immediately felt a strong need for money. A highly labour-intensive crop, cotton required a large financial outlay; the expenditure involved in the sowing of cotton was, for example, four times higher than that entailed in sowing an equivalent area with wheat. For this reason the dehkans (local peasants) found themselves resorting more and more to taking credit. The level of their indebtedness gradually reached large proportions. In regions where cotton was the main crop, as for example in the Fergana Valley, about 65% of all smallholdings resorted to credit (moreover, credit was given only if the crop to be sown was cotton)[76]. Credit was given by both native and Russian capital, and creditor and buyer of cotton were often one and the same person. Widespread giving of credit to the dehkans was not merely a further factor strengthening the tendency towards a cotton monoculture; it also led to an unprecedented increase in usury and, as a result, to the decline of peasant husbandry. By 1909, sparked off by the decline of dehkan farming, a long and smouldering crisis had set in the cotton-producing regions. This was attributed by the 'Bulletin of the Cotton Committee' to the growth of peasant indebtedness to money-lenders, which had led to the impoverishment of peasant smallholdings, making impossible the purchase of fertilizers and proper cultivation of the cotton fields[77]. Russian industrial capital, anxious for the fate of the cotton-producing base, began to look for a way out of the dead-end situation in which Central Asian agriculture now found itself. Interest in Turkestan began to intensify; inquiries and investigations were conducted. The most important of these was the commission led by Senator Palen, which put the main blame for the unsatisfactory state of the region's agriculture on usury. 'In order to preserve Turkestan as a colony capable of supplying us with goods and as a major market for the products of European Russia's manufacturing industry,' wrote Palen, ' it is necessary to rescue the native population from the hands of usurers and creditors'[78]. In an attempt to bring to an end the crisis in Central Asian cotton production, the Russian authorities tried to set up special loan-making funds giving cheap credit; such funds were seen as a means of saving cotton farmers from the hands of the usurers. Much hope was also placed upon the import of cheap wheat from Russia. In opposition to this, a report issued by the Russian Ministry of Agriculture declared that neither cheap credit nor correct agronomic methods could substitute for the necessity of bringing new land under irrigation for cotton production[79]. The Russian government, however, withheld its consent to concessions for the construction of irrigation systems from both Russian and foreign businessmen, in the belief that the irrigation of large areas of Turkestan was a matter to be decided at national and state level. As history was to show, though, the Turkestan government itself did nothing.

From the beginning of the 20th century cotton began to play a dominant role in the economic life of Central Asia; its importance continued to grow right up to the October Revolution of 1917. By the beginning of the First World War in 1914, for example, on the territory of modern Uzbekistan cotton had supplanted all other crops, and in the more advanced agricultural regions more than half of the area under crops was planted with cotton[80]. Nevertheless, until the First World War imported American cotton made up a significant proportion of cotton consumed by Russia; competition from America had an unfavourable effect on the Central Asian cotton producers. The overproduction of cotton in the USA and the reduction of world cotton prices in 1911, for example, badly affected the internal Russian market, knocking down the price of Central Asian cotton. The First World War gave new impetus to cotton production in Central Asia. As imports of the raw material were cut back, the importance of Central Asian cotton grew, as did it its price. If at the beginning of the war 50% of Russia's cotton need was supplied by Central Asia, by the end of the war this figure had grown to almost 100%. However, it was cotton that became one of the causes of the major anti-Russian uprising in Central Asia in 1916. The expansion of the area of agricultural land planted with cotton had occurred not as a result of an increase in the overall area of irrigated land, but by means of a reduction in the area of land planted with grain crops, and this led to deficits in food produce, and to increases in the price of food. Whilst the Russian administration was prepared to pay high prices for cotton, the native peasants put up with food shortages caused by cotton fever and by the war; but when the Tsar's government set fixed and artificially low prices for cotton, they revolted.

Until the October Revolution of 1917 the only relatively developed sector of industry in Central Asia was the cotton industry, which produced 80% of the entire industrial production of the region[81].

The Soviet Policy of the Monoculture of Cotton

The establishment of Soviet rule in Central Asia did nothing to change the region's specialization in cotton; rather, the opposite: proceeding from the strategic military and economic interests of the new ideology, the central leadership of the Communist Party placed even more importance on the production of cotton in the region. According to the ideological axioms of Marxist-Leninism, socialist industrialization begins with the creation of heavy industry - and not with light industry, as was the case in the countries of the West during the industrial revolution. In Central Asia, however, this particular ideological dogma was betrayed by the communists, who, working from a principle of maximum growth of cotton production, put most emphasis on sectors of industry capable of facilitating the production of cotton. Right up to the beginning of the Second World War, for example, in Uzbekistan - the most advanced of the cotton-producing republics - heavy industry made up no more than 14% of the region's industry. This tendency was reversed during the war years, when the forced evacuation of machine-manufacturing factories from Western regions to Central

Asia and defence needs laid the foundations of the rapid development of heavy industry in the region.

Until the disintegration of the USSR cotton production remained the main economic sector of the majority of the Central Asian republics. Cotton production became the focus for the development of a large economic complex embracing many industrial sectors: irrigation; production of agricultural machinery; production of mineral fertilizers and toxic chemicals; the cotton-refining, oil-producing, paper-manufacturing and - to a lesser extent - sewing and knitting industries. By the beginning of the 1990s the annual cotton harvest had reached approximately 8 million tons (i.e. 17% of total world cotton production), and supplied more than 90% of the USSR's cotton requirements. Three quarters of the total Central Asian cotton crop was produced by Uzbekistan, followed at a large distance by Tadjikistan and Turkmenistan, whose cotton harvests were approximately of identical size - around 1 million tons[82]. By the 1980s the Central Asian republics (with the exception of Kazakhstan) had achieved the maximum level of cotton production possible given the existing water resources and the technological condition of the region's irrigation systems. The specific gravity of cotton-planting (cottonization) had reached 70%. Cotton had practically usurped all grain crops, and had taken over land used in the past for the cultivation of fruit and vegetables; it had become the only crop grown in the majority of kolkhozes and sovkhozes. It is interesting to note that on the very eve of the disintegration of the USSR Gorbachev cited Uzbekistan as a classic example of total specialization in cotton production; this, according to Gorbachev, was no cause for alarm provided that there existed a unified Soviet state[83]. The unique level of cottonization in Central Asia had given rise to serious economic, social and even ecological problems. Amongst these particular emphasis should be given

114

to the acute shortage of food crops in the region. Central Asia, a territory favoured with fertile land and a wonderful climate, suffers from an insufficiency of vegetables, fruits, wheat, meat and milk. If even before the disintegration of the USSR imports of produce from other regions were insufficient, as a result of the disruption of economic relations the situation at the present time is still worse. No less serious is the shortage of water, caused by excessive cottonization. In Central Asian condition successful cultivation of cotton is possible only on irrigated land and with a large supply of water. But by the middle of the 1980s the Central Asian republics had already almost exhausted all their water resources - resources which were exceedingly limited even without the extra demands made upon them by cotton production. The waters of the rivers Zeravshan, Kashkadarya, Murgab and Tedzhen are entirely used up in irrigating the cotton fields, and fail to reach the Amudarya, into which they previously used to fall. The natural regime of Central Asia's two largest rivers - the Amudarya and the Syrdarya - has also been severely disturbed, reducing these rivers' outflow into the Aral Sea by at least three quarters[84]. The Syrdarya itself stopped reaching the sea as far back as the middle of the 1970s - all its water being dispersed through irrigation systems. An indicator of the catastrophic position with water resources in Central Asia is the problem of the dehydration of the Aral Sea. Over the 30 years (1960-90) the sea's water level has fallen by almost 14 metres; its surface area has been reduced by 40%, whilst its water volume has fallen by 65%. The average salinity of the sea has increased 2.5 times, and the sea has lost all its value to the fishing industry[85]. As a result of high expenditure of water on cotton, water shortages have started to affect both industry and the ordinary population.

The intensive use of toxic chemicals on the cotton fields has in many places led to systematic poisoning of drinking water, to pollution of the environment and, as a consequence, to increases in levels of sickness amongst the native population. Before the break-up of the USSR toxic chemicals were being used in Central Asia at a rate of 20 - 25kg per hectare, whilst the average rate throughout the former Soviet Union was 3kg per hectare. As a result, levels of infection with viral hepatitis and other diseases caused by pollution of the environment are 3 - 5 times higher than in Russia. For example, in the Vakhsh Valley of Tadjikistan, an area with a population of one million at the present time, little more than 30% of inhabitants have tap-water; in the main people drink polluted water from irrigation ditches fed with water running off the cotton fields[86]. As a result of the thoughtless use of fertilizer - exceeding amounts required by 50 times - the earth on many cotton fields has become covered with a thin layer of salts and chemicals. Almost all women working in the fields have suffered from a variety of illnesses caused by pollution of the environment.

During 'perestroika' and 'glasnost' the Central Asian press openly condemned yet another unpleasant consequence of the excessive cottonization of Central Asia - the common use of child labour. 'The slogan of cotton independence,' wrote the paper 'Kommunist Tadjikistana', 'concealed the forcible methods used in introducing this industrial crop. Receiving peanuts for work of the most demanding kind, fathers of families were forced to seek additional ways of earning money, and would send their wives and children to take their places in the cotton fields. And this state of affairs continues to the present day. As a result we have a most shameful phenomenon - child labour. This has deprived the larger part of the native inhabitants of the cotton republics of even the barely adequate education they would otherwise have received[87]'. According to the local press, the extremely low level of education was to blame for the fact that Central Asians called up to serve in the army were fit only for special battalions engaged in construction work, as well as for the fact that local professionals were significantly less good at their job than professionals of other nationalities[88]. Central Asian sociologists are of the opinion that the cotton monoculture was also responsible for preserving a feudal structure and traditional society in the region. These sociologists see the compulsory cultivation of cotton at ridiculously low prices as a form of corvee - an element of the feudal system of management. Another aspect they see as characteristic of the feudal community is wage-levelling, a system which was applied intensively in the cotton-growing kolkhozes. Wage-levelling, a relic of the barrack socialism professed by the very first socialists - the utopianists Owen, Saint-Simon and Fourier - was put into practice by the Bolsheviks in the USSR. Being genetically close to feudal wage-levelling, the wage-levelling of barrack socialism easily entered the mass consciousness of the Central Asian peoples. The feudal community, of course, strove to maintain equality of income between its members[89].

On the eve of the disintegration of the Soviet Union glaring contradictions emerged between the interests of the centre, which called for cotton production to be increased, and the economic and social needs of Central Asia, needs which dictated a reduction of cotton planting. By 1989 cotton production in the main cotton republic, Uzbekistan, had reached approximately 5 million tons. The centre wanted to increase production to 6 million tons, but the local Uzbek management, in conditions of incomparably greater 'glasnost' than earlier, asked for permission to cut back cotton production. Uzbek academics and public figures likewise called for the republic's excessive cottonization to be reduced. Local specialists, and in particular the academic M. Mukhametdzhanov, pointed out that reductions in cotton production would allow the elimination of shortages of food produce, especially in view of the fact that consumption of meat, milk, vegetables and fruit per head of population in Uzbekistan was 2 - 2.5 times lower than the average for the country as a whole, whilst the republic's national income was two times lower than the average income for the Soviet Union[90]. Nevertheless, the situation remained essentially unchanged until the disintegration of the USSR in 1991, due to the fact that the prices fixed by the centre for agricultural production and the high level of unemployment made cuts in cotton production unprofitable for the Central Asian republics. The high birth-rate amongst the peoples of Central Asia - approximately 3% per year i.e. five times higher than in Russia or the Baltic states - leads to a yearly reduction in the area of irrigated land per head of population (the present 0.2 hectares per head will fall to 0.16 hectares per head in the near future). For this reason the Central Asian republics are forced to develop production of crops which are maximally labour-intensive and profit-yielding, such as cotton, grapes and tobacco. All other conditions being equal, cotton production is capable of providing 30 times more jobs than production of grain; four times more jobs than cultivation of vegetables, and three times more jobs than cultivation of fruits[91]. In view of the fact that even according to official figures there were in 1990, in Uzbekistan alone, more than one million unemployed (out of a total population of 20 million), unemployment in agriculture had to be treated as an urgent problem. In conditions where prices set by the centre for agricultural produce were clearly artificially low, cotton remained one of the most profitable crops. Production of cotton was, for example, four times more profitable than cultivation of wheat. Thus the Soviet government followed the example of its imperial predecessor in using a pricing policy to stimulate cotton production in Central Asia. The results of this single-minded economic policy exceeded all expectation. If the average annual cotton yield of the territory covered by modern Uzbekistan was around 100 000 tons before the October Revolution of 1917, by the time of the disintegration of the USSR it was 50 times greater. Allowance has to be made, of course, for the fact that, unlike the pre-Revolutionary Russian administration, the Soviet communist leadership resorted to non-economic measures of compulsion, forcing managers of kolkhozes and sovkhozes to increase cotton production at whatever cost and sell it to the Soviet state at prices significantly lower than cost price. As a result of this the cotton-producers of Uzbekistan in the course of a mere five years (1984 - 1988) were, according to the estimates of Central Asian economists (amongst them economists of Russian origin), underpaid a sum of 14.6 billion roubles; this, it should be said, was at a time when the rouble had not yet been rendered valueless by hyperinflation[92]. Right up until 1991 the Soviet authorities were still forcing sales of cotton at the ridiculously low price of 810 roubles per ton, when, according to calculations by specialists, the price should have been more than 2700 roubles per ton[93]. It is worth noting that in pre-Revolutionary times Russian merchants paid their Uzbek suppliers 18 poods of wheat for one pood of cotton, and for a ton of raw cotton paid 556 golden roubles - a sum many times greater than the modern-day price. During the years of 'perestroika' and 'glasnost' Central Asian society many times debated the need to put an end to the compulsory sale of cotton to the state for prices so low that they amounted to robbery. But for as long as the Soviet Union remained intact Central Asia had no real chance of breaking out of the vice of the cotton monoculture and low cotton prices without significant changes being made to the entire economic system of the USSR. Even during the time of Gorbachev's reforms the prevailing point of view continued to be that the Soviet economy should have its own pricing system independent of prices on the international markets. In practice this meant a policy of isolation of the Soviet Union from the world economy - a policy which had a damaging effect on the Soviet economy's competitiveness.

'The Cotton Case'

The turning of the Central Asian republics into a raw-material-producing appendix of the centre; the compulsory measures employed by the central structures in order to maximize production of cheap cotton; the arbitrary decision-making, corruption and incestuousness rife amongst the local power structures - all this paved the way for the so-called 'cotton case', which began as far back as 1983, under the brief rule of Andropov, but finished going through the courts only as the USSR was in the process of disintegrating. The 'cotton case' was a massive fraud centring on supplies of cotton and involving, as it transpired, the majority of the Uzbek Party leadership during the rule of the Uzbekistan First Secretary, Rashidov. Crude pressure applied to the kolkhozes in an attempt to force them to go to all lengths in order to raise their yields to 30 centners per hectare (when a realistic yield would have been no more than 25 centners per hectare) led to the local leadership reporting false and distortedly high results. As later emerged, the breathtaking records achieved by the Uzbek cotton-producers were breathtaking lies. In actual fact the republic's kolkhozes and sovkhozes produced only a part of the quantity of cotton recorded in accounts submitted to the centre. The 9 million tons of 'white gold' reported by Central Asian Party leaders at the beginning of the 1980s turned out to be a massive falsification. Even according to the official figures - which are almost certainly too low - in Uzbekistan alone results were distorted upwards by more than

600,000 tons of cotton, costing the USSR hundreds of millions of roubles in losses every year[94]. In the course of investigations 3,000 police employees were dismissed from their posts; 4,000 local Party functionaries were sent for trial; and the initiators of the fraud were sentenced to death. Many Uzbek managers in high positions committed suicide, whilst others, such as Rashidov, met early deaths in mysterious circumstances. The 'cotton case' provoked active intervention in Uzbek and Central Asian affairs by the centre - first under Andropov, then under Gorbachev. The Central Committee of the Communist Party took a decision to 'reinforce' the Central Asian party organizations and in order to 'improve the health' of the republic dispatched a large number of Party and economic officials from the centre[95]. This in turn led to a flaring-up of nationalism among many layers of Central Asian society, and to open questioning, for the first time during Soviet rule, of the Russification of the region. The court cases resulting from the investigation into the affair went on right up till the time of the USSR's disintegration, putting a strain on relations between Russians and Uzbeks. Only after Uzbekistan had declared its independence did President Karimov rehabilitate almost all those convicted; in this way he closed the case once and for all, allowing it to be understood that the true criminals were sitting in Moscow.

The Geography of Cotton and the Water Shortage

As far as concerns climatic and geographic conditions necessary for the growing of cotton, Uzbekistan has a significant advantage over all other republics. As is well-known, cotton can be cultivated on land up to a height of 1200m above sea level, whilst the greater part of Tadjikistan is more than 3000m above sea level.

The mountainous republic of Kyrgyzstan is in a similar position. In distinction to the latter two republics, Turkmenistan consists mostly of level land, but these plains are almost entirely occupied by the waterless and sandy Karakum desert. Cotton-cultivation is also impossible throughout most of Kazakhstan - which makes up the entire northern part of Central Asia - due to the cold climate and shortage of water. Kazakhstan's agriculture differs in important structural ways from the specialization of the other Central Asian republics: here the main role is played by cattle and farming based on grain crops, whilst cotton-cultivation is practised only in Chimkentskaya oblast (province). For this reason Kazakhstan was in 1961 designated as a separate economic district amongst the USSR's network of economic districts. Southern Kazakhstan, though - i.e. Chimkentskaya, Dzhambulskaya and Alma-Atinskaya oblasts (provinces) - is in natural and economic characteristics similar to the other four Central Asian republics. Since in the arid conditions of Central Asia cotton-cultivation is mainly feasible on irrigated land, the majority of cotton planted is concentrated in the Fergana and Zeravshan Valleys of Uzbekistan. Uzbekistan, considered as a whole, contains the greater part of irrigated land in Central Asia, whilst Central Asian irrigated land made up almost half of all irrigated land in the USSR.

In spite of the predominance in Central Asia of deserts and mountains, the main agricultural problem in the region is not lack of land suitable for cultivation, but the serious shortage of water for irrigation. In four Central Asian republics alone - i.e. not including Kazakhstan - the quantity of land available for cultivation comes to approximately 25 million hectares, which is significantly more than can be provided for by the irrigational capacity of all the Central Asian rivers taken together[96]. However, even such water resources as Central Asia does have are distributed highly unevenly: 80% of such resources are enjoyed by Kyrgyzstan and Tadjikistan, republics which have little land suitable for the cultivation of cotton, whilst Uzbekistan and Turkmenistan, which have the greater part of such suitable land, receive only 20% of total water resources.

The main consumers of water in the region are the irrigation systems serving the cotton fields. Loss of water in such systems is, however, very large, and amounts to an average of between a half and two thirds of all water used. Thus it is not merely the shortage of water that is a serious problem in cotton production, but also non-rational use of water.

Another agricultural problem in Central Asia has become the loss of a large area of land, as a result of the senseless use of former prime agricultural land for urban development. This negates all efforts to bring new land for cotton under irrigation. In the years 1961 - 1969, for instance, approximately one million hectares of new irrigated land (out of a total of 1.3 million over the whole of the USSR) were brought into exploitation in Central Asia, and yet the overall area of land under irrigation increased by a mere 93 000 hectares[97]. In the opinion of specialists, it would make far more sense to put resources invested in irrigating new land into improving the already-existing irrigation systems and to reducing water loss in such systems. At the same time, however, leading hydrologists warn that the transition from a cotton monoculture to other agricultural crops cannot lead to a significant reduction in water-consumption. Scientifically established irrigation norms for the majority of food crops are no lower than that for cotton. For this reason, the hydrologists affirm, the proposed measures for reducing cotton-planting make sense only from the point of view of solving the problem of food production[98]. The only radical solution of Central Asia's water shortage problem would be the realization of a project to divert part of the flow of the Siberian rivers. A project of this kind was drawn up, but met with telling objections from both environmental movements and local populations (in areas of Siberia from which water would be diverted) alike. The disintegration of the Soviet Union made realization of this project impossible.

The Central Asian Formula

Before the break-up of the USSR half of all Central Asian cotton was harvested using machines. The inefficiency of these cotton combine-harvesters, however, made it necessary, as a rule, for manual labour to be used to complete the harvesting of the cotton. In addition, the use of agricultural machinery entailed increased use of herbicides - in order to eliminate green leaves hindering the work of the combines, for instance; this naturally had a very damaging effect both on the environment and on the health of the local population. In the past few years, though, in an attempt to reduce unemployment in rural areas and halt pollution of the environment, the local government has stopped encouraging use of machinery, and the level of mechanization in cotton production has accordingly dropped. The severance of economic links following the events of 1991 caused a serious shortage of spare parts, rendering much agricultural machinery disabled and leading to a further reduction in the level of mechanization in Central Asia. Thus poor mechanization and a low level of productivity from labour are characteristic of Central Asian agriculture as it is today; Central Asia suffers from low profitability. Incidentally, even before the break-up of the USSR 75% of all kolkhozes and sovkhozes were either openly loss-making or had difficulty in making ends meet. Private smallholdings, however, occupying a mere 4% of irrigated land, produced more than a quarter of all agricultural produce. Following the declaration of independence by Central Asian states, much hope was placed on the development of these smallholdings. But initial euphoria at the prospects offered by private farming gave way to more sober evaluation. Central Asian peasants, as it has transpired, have no particular desire for independence. In Kazakhstan, the largest Central Asian republic, for example, there are, according to figures published by the journal 'Ekonomika i zhizn', a mere 9,400 independent farmers possessing only 2.2% of arable land and 1.3% of pastureland. Of those who could join the ranks of the independent farmers, 80% fear having to confront their problems on their own, whilst 78% additionally lack the necessary finance[99]. In another Central Asian republic, Turkmenistan, where land reform is proceeding at a more active rate, the number of private farmers is only a little higher (11,000); these farmers have been allotted land which previously lay empty[100]. The slow rate of agrarian reform in Central Asia is accounted for by the desire of the old communist leadership of the region to preserve social and economic structures, such as kolkhozes and sovkhozes, over which they have full control. On the other hand, the years of forcible collectivization and mass repressions combined with the arbitrary decision-making and corruption of the local administration have stripped the peasantry of all initiative for a long time to come. Thus the social and economic situation in Central Asia continues, even after the break-up of the USSR, to be defined by the following sad formula: the lowest labour productivity in the former Soviet Union against a background of the lowest living standard and the highest birth rate. In agriculture the situation is aggravated by chronic problems such as unemployment, a serious shortage of water and environmental pollution.

Prospects

The formation of the independent Central Asian states has given urgency to the question of the exploitation of the cotton harvest. Until the break-up of the USSR 92% of all Central Asian cotton was sent for processing to the central regions of Russia. What remained was allotted to the small local textile industry. At the present time, however, the entire cotton harvest remains the property of the Central Asian republics, but is exported almost in its entirety since Central Asia itself lacks a sufficiently-developed textile manufacturing base; cotton is now the main source of hard currency for the Central Asia republics. In 1992 Uzbekistan became the second largest exporter of cotton on the world market after the USA, whilst Russia has become the largest importer in the world. A significant proportion of Central Asian cotton continues to make its way into Russia as before, in exchange for supplies of Russian oil, gas and timber. This kind of exchange, though, is unprofitable for the Russian importers. Firstly, the Central Asian republics have shown themselves to be unreliable suppliers, falling seriously behind with supplies of cotton to Russia. Secondly, Russia finds that cotton from this source is costing it too much. In spite of the fact that transactions should now be carried out at world prices and Central Asian cotton is worth comparatively little, Russia in 1992 paid 15 tons of oil for every ton of cotton. Now if Russia decided to buy Californian cotton - which is better than Central Asian in terms of quality - it would find the change of supplier one and a half times more profitable. At the same time, however, although in 1993 - 1994 the government of the Russian Federation gave serious consideration to refusing supplies of Central Asian cotton, it refrained from doing so for reasons of a political character. The Central Asian states are the most compliant members of the Commonwealth of Independent States; Russia will undoubtedly continue to pay for their complaisance with sacrifices of its economic interests in the future.

The last decade has seen the discovery of major gas and oil deposits in Turkmenistan and Uzbekistan, such as could in the future become an alternative source of hard currency to cotton. In the immediate future, however, there is unlikely to be any diminution of the importance of cotton for the Central Asian states since there is no sufficient system by which oil and gas could be supplied to potential consumers abroad. Substantial investment is needed in order to build oil- and gas-pipes, but western investors are in no hurry to come forward due to the lack of political stability in the area. In addition, arguments continue to rage over alternatives for the routes to be taken by the gas- and oil-pipes; such arguments are a direct consequence of the struggle for spheres of influence between neighbours in Central Asia. Thus it has to be supposed that the Central Asian states will for a long time to come be unable to permit themselves to make cuts in cotton-production; cotton continues to remain the most important commodity, and the only commodity bringing in hard currency through export sales. In view of the poor competitiveness of Central Asian cotton (in comparison with American or Egyptian), it is evident that cotton will be one more in the array of factors consolidating Central Asia's dependence on Russia. Thus, in imposing on Central Asia the cotton monoculture, in bringing about an economic revolution to suit the interests of cotton production in complete isolation from the world market, Russia has left behind a heavy inheritance from which the Central Asian states are in no condition to free themselves without outside help in the near future.

Chapter Five

THE DETERIORATION OF THE ECOLOGICAL SITUATION: CAUSES AND POSSIBLE CONSEQUENCES

The Area Around the Aral Sea on the Eve of Ecological Catastrophe

The ecological and social and economic processes occurring in the region of the Aral Sea today give every reason to call the area an ecological catastrophe zone. In the last thirty years the Aral Sea's water level has fallen by 14 metres; its surface area has suffered a reduction of 40%; the volume of its water mass has dropped by 65%; and its average salinity has increased 2.5 times[101]. The Aral Sea previously yielded 7% of all fish caught in the former USSR; now it has no value for the fishing industry whatsoever. In many places the sea has retreated by 70 - 100km from its previous shores, leaving ports stranded far from its waters; navigation has almost entirely ceased[102]. The desiccation of the Aral Sea has left tens of thousands of people without work. The area of land left uncovered by the sea now exceeds 2 milllion hectares, and has become a breeding ground for salt storms. There has been a marked deterioration in the climate, making productive agriculture impossible in the coastal regions. The Aral Sea region is divided roughly equally between two Central Asian states - Kazakhstan and Uzbekistan - and has a population of approximately 3 million. Worst off of all are the inhabitants of the autonomous republic of Karakalpakiya, which is a part of Uzbekistan. In the words of a Karakalpakiyan parliamentary deputy 'What the Karakalpakiyan people are going through today is nothing short of a tragedy. 70% of the population are ill; the republic has not a single maternity hospital; there's a shortage of housing, a lack of drinkable drinking water; as a result of malnutrition, women cannot feed their baby children ... No other area of the country (the former USSR) has a situation like this - this is an ecological catastrophe.'[103]

The unrestrained use of mineral fertilizers on the soil has led to a situation in which irrigated land has become not merely polluted, but a source of pollution for the environment. The waters of the Amudarya and Syrdarya, which issue into the Aral Sea, have been found to contain chemical fertilizers and high concentrations of harmful components from heavy metals, cancerogens and harmful bacteria. Due to the lack of other sources of fresh water, a large part of the population of the Republic of Karakalpakia and of Kzyl-Orda and Chimkent oblasts (provinces) continues to use water unfit for domestic use. But there is a deficit of even such unsuitable water too; water use in the region is 5 - 6 times lower than average. As a result of this, the overall death-rate in the region has in the last 25 years increased two-fold, and infant mortality has risen from 44.7 per 1000 births in 1965 to 71.5 per 1000 in 1986 (and, in places, to 80 – 90 per 1000). Karakalpakia for a long time had the highest birth-rate in the USSR; now - amongst the countries of the former Soviet Union - it has the highest death-rate. Almost 90% of 1 - 2 month-old children seen by local hospitals are found to have urine whose salinity is far in excess of the norm. Throughout the Aral Sea region incidence of enteric typhoid has increased 30 times; incidence of infection with viral hepatitis has increased 7 times; there has been a significant increase in the level of tuburcular and and oncological illness (15 times higher than the average for the former USSR) [104].

The main reason for the rapid desiccation of the Aral Sea and its surrounding region is the the excessive drawing-off of water for irrigation purposes from the Amuradya and Syrdarya rivers, which come out into the Aral Sea. The middle of the 1960s saw the start of an intensive campaign throughout Central Asia, but particularly in Uzbekistan, to bring new territory under cultivation. In the period between 1965 and the end of the 1980s, the region's stock of fertile land increased almost twofold, from 2.3 million to 4.2 million hectares [105]. As a result, there was a sharp increase in the volume of water drawn off from the two main rivers in Central Asia - the Amudarya and the Syrdarya - as well as from their tributaries. The waters of the rivers Zeravshan, Tedzhen, Kashkadarya and Murgab, for instance, which until recently used to fall into the Amudarya, are now entirely consumed by irrigation processes and no longer reach the Amudarya. The Syrdarya, the second largest river in Central Asia, used to have a flow of 34 cubic kilometres of water per year; in 1989 it contributed to the Aral Sea little more than 3 cubic kilometres. Meanwhile, the largest Central Asian river, the Amudarya, whose average annual flow in the not so distant past was 75 - 78 cubic kilometres [106], now gives the Aral not a litre, its waters disappearing in their entirety into irrigational systems feeding the cotton fields. These figures have to be considered in the light of the fact that, simply in order to maintain the present state of the Aral Sea, an annual supply of 35 - 40 cubic kilometres of water is required.

It has to be admitted that the impending ecological catastrophe in the Aral Sea region met with concern and alarm not only amongst society at large, but amongst the Central Asian governments as well. Moreover, discussion about the necessity of saving the Aral Sea drew in government bodies in Moscow, and spread to central newspapers and publications; a broad-based 'Aral movement' sprang up. Neither amongst society or government bodies, however, did this activity result in the taking of a decisive decision. This was due, on the one hand, to the huge cost of work necessary to save the Aral Sea - a cost which was beyond the pockets of the Central Asian republics and which required considerable financial support from the centre - and, on the other hand, to opposition from society and local authorities in other regions of the USSR unwilling to make financial sacrifices or to take cutbacks in natural resources for the sake of a solution to Central Asian problems. Under the official programme for saving the Aral Sea (developed on the eve of the break-up of the Soviet Union), reconstruction work on existing irrigation systems was to lead to an increase in the flow of water into the Aral to 21 - 22 cubic kilometres by the end of the 20th century. This, of course, was too little - and too late - to save the sea. For even if this programme were to have been carried out in full, the Aral would have ceased to exist, being replaced by several small lakes. The break-up of the USSR, however, made even this modest plan impossible to implement.

The animated discussion concerning the impending ecological catastrophe revealed two very different points of view. According to the first of these, the Aral Sea should be allowed to dry up completely and all water needed for its salvation given over to agricultural requirements, since only an increase in cotton production can compensate for losses resulting from the destruction of the sea. According to the second point of view, the desiccation of the Aral Sea should be prevented at whatever cost, since its disappearance would lead to ecological catastrophe not merely in the Aral Sea region but over the greater part of Central Asia as well. An important argument in the armoury of those who are ready to accept the disappearance of the Aral is provided by Central Asian history. There is entirely reliable historical evidence which tells us that the Aral Sea and its water level have been subject to periodic changes of a marked character in accordance with changes in the direction of flow of the River Amudarya. In the course of human history there have been three variations in the flow of the river:

1. its entire flow has discharged into the Caspian Sea;

2. its entire flow has discharged into the Aral Sea;

3. the larger part of its flow has discharged into the Caspian, the lesser part into the Aral.

These facts have allowed hydrological specialists to declare that the desiccation of the Aral Sea is a cyclical process, as well as to cast doubt upon the existence of the sea in the remote past. According to the latter version, put forward by specialists from the State Hydrological Institute (St Petersburg) in 1994, changes in the volume of flow of rivers in the basin of the Aral and Caspian Seas are to be explained not by precipitation, but by processes occurring in the bowels of the earth. Russian hydrologists involved in research in Central Asia are of the opinion that the present period is one of increasing tension in the earth's crust in the region of the Caspian Sea. As a result of increases of tension along fissures a huge quantity of subterranean water is being squeezed out into rivers and seas. This explains why over the last fifteen years the water level of the Caspian Sea has risen at an average speed of 15cm/year. The excess of water which has accumulated in the Caspian Sea now exceeds 600 cubic kilometres[107]. In 1992, in order to get rid of this undesired accumulation of water, the dam (built 12 years earlier) separating the Caspian from the Gulf of Kara-Bogaz-Gol was knocked down. The Gulf had been compared with a 'black maw', continually sucking in the waters of the Caspian Sea. In spite of the dam's destruction and the fact that the Gulf is now full, the water level in the Caspian has not gone down. The rising waters of the Caspian Sea flood coastal lands under cultivation, wash away agricultural constructions and housing, and impede drilling operations and the work of the oil industry. If the Caspian Sea region is experiencing a compression resulting in an upward movement of subterranean waters, the earth's crust in the region around the Aral Sea should, according to Russian hydrologists, be undergoing expansion, leading to a downward flow of water into subterranean reservoirs. Russian specialists estimate that in the Aral basin over the last two decades 15 cubic kilometres of water have disappeared every year[108]. Attention has also been drawn to the fact that the fall in the sea level has been accompanied by a significant reduction in the flow of water off the mountains; this water is not used for irrigation purposes. Attempts to explain this by a reduction in precipitation in the mountains proved unsuccessful; far from declining, quantity of precipitation has in fact increased. Numerous investigations over recent years have led to the conclusion that the region of the Aral Sea is subject to a periodic natural process causing a reflux of water from rivers, lakes and the sea back into subterranean reservoirs. It follows from this hypothesis that the flow of water will be reversed only when seismic processes die down and there is a drop in the number and force of earthquakes along the channels of the Amudarya and Syrdarya.

From the History of Central Asian Geography

Investigations into geological deposits and geographical forma-
tions on the slopes of the Sarykamysh depression, which lies between the Aral and the Caspian Seas, have shown that during the
last few thousand years this depression has alternately filled with
water and dried up. During wet periods the depression has been
the site of a freshwater lake - the Sarykamysh Lake - with a depth
of more than 100m; the shores of this lake have been densely populated with human beings. The Sarykamysh Lake was joined, by
means of a river, which has since dried up, to both the Caspian and
the Amudarya. It is assumed that the old delta of the Amudarya
was attached not to the Aral Sea, but to the Sarykamysh depression itself. In the distant past the waters of the Amudarya would
flow (wholly or partially) along the now dried-up channel first into
the Sarykamysh depression, and subsequently, emerging from the
lake, into the Caspian Sea. This dried-up channel is today called
the Uzboi. There is a large quantity of evidence to support the view
that in the past the Uzboi was a proper river and that the waters
of the Amudarya flowed, in the main, not into the Aral, but into
the Caspian Sea. The earliest of this evidence is from the time of
Alexander of Macedon's march into Central Asia. Alexander the
Great's companion Aristobul states that at that time the Amudarya
(in Greek, the Oxus) flowed into the Girkan Sea (the Caspian), that
it was navigable and was used by ships carrying goods from India
through the Caspian and thence through mountain passes to the
Black Sea[109]. During Genghis Khan's conquest of Central Asia, the
Mongols broke the resistance of the foe by knocking down dams
on the Amudarya, causing that river's waters to escape from the
irrigation network and surge westwards following the old channel

left over from the ice age - first to Sarykamysh, then to the Caspian Sea. The same period saw the beginning of the desiccation of the northern part of the delta around the Aral Sea. In 1339, in an essay with the title 'Comfort for hearts', the geographer Khamdallakh Kazvini wrote that several channels of the Dzheikhun (Amudarya) flowed out into the Khorezm Lake (Aral Sea), whilst the river's main branch passed through Khorezm into the Khazar (Caspian) Sea. Still more striking is that, according to the same geographer, a branch of the Amydarya-Uzboi which flowed into the Caspian had a current so strong that the roar of its waterfalls could be heard for a distance of 10 - 15 km. The now desiccated Uzboi in those times watered a large and plentiful land, which survives today only in the form of city ruins and the remains of ancient canals crossing the desert. The medieval chronicler Zakhir-ad-din tells us that where the Uzboi flowed into the Caspian Sea there stood the city of Agrycha, and that it was from this city that in 1392 Timur gave orders for the captive masters of Mazendaran to be taken on ships upstream on the Amudarya. All this historical evidence supports what we know from geology, i.e. that in ancient times and during the Middle Ages a branch of the Amudarya (the main branch, it has to be supposed) issued not into the Aral, but into the Caspian Sea. Many medieval geographical maps show the Amudarya having two branches - one connecting with the Aral Sea, the other with the Caspian; this picture was corrected by later geographers who, aware of the extreme confusion inherent in medieval cartography, concluded that it must be false.

To the present day we do not know when the course of the Uzboi dried up, and when the Amudarya's link with the Caspian Sea was broken. The shores of the Sarykamysh Lake preserve signs of a gradual drop in water level; areas surrounding the lake were settled by farmers who constructed irrigation systems and complicated machinery for raising water onto the fields. However the lake (occupying an area of 12 000 square kilometres in the Sarykamysh depression) quickly went dry, aided to a certain extent by the rulers of the Khiva Khanate (Khorezm), who used their control over the river as a method of enforcing the obedience of Turkmen tribes dependent on the passage of water through the Uzboi. At the very beginning of the 18th century the Turkmens, convinced that Khiva was intending to prevent the westward flow of water in the Amudarya, turned to the Russian Tsar Peter I with a plea for help. The Turkmen ambassador was able to convince Peter that destruction of the dams built by the Khiva khans would give the Russian merchant fleet a direct route, through the Uzboi, into Central Asia and thence to India. As a result of negotiations with the Turkmens, Peter I dispatched an expedition under the leadership of Prince Alexander Bekovich-Cherkasskiy to the shores of the Caspian Sea and the estuary of the Uzboi. In 1714 the Russian expedition located the point at which the Uzboy issued into the Caspian Sea, and (for the first time) established with absolute certainty that the western, i.e. Caspian, channel of the Amudarya had dried up; how long the channel had been in that condition before the arrival of the Russian expedition can only be guessed at. The existing historical evidence allows us to state one more conclusion: during times of peace, when irrigation systems would be in full use, the greater part of the Amudarya's water flowed into the Aral Sea and the lesser part into the Caspian; conversely, during times of war and when the irrigation systems were in a state of ruin or during years of heavy rainfall, the greater volume of water issued through the Sarykamysh and Uzboi into the Caspian Sea. This was the situation at the time of the invasion of Genghis Khan at the beginning of the 13th century and during the ravaging expeditions led by Timur in the 1370s and 1380s, when first the Mongols, and then the 'Iron Limper' frequently passed through Khorezm, leaving behind them only scorched earth. At the same, however, we still do not know what is the main reason for changes in the direction of the waters of the Amudarya - action by human beings (the construction and destruction of irrigation systems) or natural factors (differing levels of water build-up at different times)? The 13th and 14th centuries, as it happens, constituted one of the wettest periods in the climatic history of Central Asia; it is possible that the high level of water concentration in the steppes played a role in the invasions of Genghis Khan, in as far as the abundance of pasture led to large increases in cattle numbers and, consequently, to similar increases in the numbers and strength of the nomads themselves. In distinction to settled peoples, the nomads depend much more on conditions in nature than on the results of their labours. In the opinion of the Russian historian and geographer L.N. Gumilev, the potential of nomadic peoples has always been in relation to changes of climate[110].

The Desiccation of Central Asia

Russian - and, subsequently, Soviet - academics were the first, and, perhaps for historical and political factors, the only specialists successful in carrying out a detailed investigation of the geology, geography and climate of Central Asia in the second half of the 19th and in the 20th centuries. The great majority of these academics (particularly in pre-Revolutionary times) held similar views, being of the opinion that Central Asia is in the grip of chronic desiccation. The famous Russian geographer and geologist I.V. Mushketov, for example, during the course of research in Turkestan in 1874 - 84, collected a large body of evidence concerning the drying up of Central Asia. He pointed to the fact that the

Aral Sea was shrinking as a result of a reduction in water running off the mountains; to the drop in the water level in Lake Issyk-Kul and other mountain lakes; to the rise in the permanent snow line in the mountains; to the encroachment of the desert upon oases[111]. Other Russian academics such as V.A Obruchev[112] and K.I. Bogdanovich put forward the view that climatic deterioration in Central Asia had become particularly noticeable during the last few centuries and decades; according to them, for example, it was the desiccation of Central Asia that was to be held responsible for the fall of the Turkmen city of Bayram-Ali, a city which had been flourishing as late as the end of the 18th century[113]. Against this, though, it has to be said that the important Russian orientalist V.V. Bartold, who conducted a thorough study of the dawn and sunset of Central Asia's numerous oases, considered the common belief in a previous abundance of water mistaken, being of the opinion that there had never been a time in the past when the whole of Central Asia had been free of water shortages[114]. In Soviet times specialists were much influenced in their conclusions by the general ideological stance taken by Marxism-Leninism, which held that the dominant factor is not nature's influence on man, but man's influence on nature; as a result, all theories regarding the desiccation of Central Asia were declared reactionary and distortive of reality. Given this basic position, Soviet scientists such as the geographer L.S. Berg[115] and the climatologist A.I. Voeikov[116] preferred to emphasize that the climate in Central Asia over the last few thousand years has been marked by relatively small fluctuations in dryness and wetness, but that no progressive climatic deterioration could be detected. During the later period of 'developed socialism' - in the works of Soviet geographers such as K.K. Markov[117], E.M. Murzaev[118] and A.G. Babaev[119], for example - credence was given to a 'compromise formula' which, on the one hand, admitted that there was a general tendency towards desiccation in Central Asia, but, on the other hand, stressed the growing influence of man over the processes of nature. At the same time, though, even the most committed opponents of the theory of desiccation in Central Asia could not deny that in both the distant past and the Middle Ages there had been much more water in the region, as is incontrovertibly shown by numerous archeological finds; 800 ancient sites, for example, have been found in the area today occupied by the Karakum and Kyzylkum deserts alone, whilst in the semi-desert regions of Ustyurt and Mangyshlak traces have been discovered of rivers and lakes which have since dried up. Experts believe that precipitation in ancient times far exceeded today's average figures[120]. Even in the medieval period there was significantly more water in Central Asia than today, and the delta of the Amudarya was more densely populated than now. In the area surrounding Kavat-Kala in Karakalpakia, for example, there were, in the 12th and 13th centuries, approximately 200 inhabitants per kilometre, a density which is roughly twice what it is today[121]. The 13th century historian Yakut confessed that he had never seen a region more densely populated and more flourishing than Khorezm.[122]

In Search of a Solution

At the present time the question of whether the drying up of Central Asia is cyclical or progressive in character has to a certain extent receded. Firstly, even if the desiccation process is cyclical, an improvement in water resources cannot be expected for many decades at the earliest. Secondly, there is no doubt that the present calamitous situation in the Aral Sea region and the imminent destruction of the Aral Sea itself are caused not by natural factors, but by Man and his activities on an economic level. Thirdly, the high birth-rate amongst the population of the Central Asian republics and the rapidly increasing needs of agriculture and industry require more and more water, which is not to be found in Central Asia itself. Even if the seemingly inevitable desiccation of the Aral Sea were to be allowed to happen, and all water needed for the sea's salvation directed towards agriculture, the problem of the Central Asian water deficit would not be solved. This is why, in spite of the catastrophic nature of the situation in the area surrounding the Aral Sea, the main ecological problem of the region as a whole is not so much the danger of the sea drying up as the threat of a growing shortage of fresh water in Central Asia - a shortage which in the future is quite capable of paralyzing the region's economy and bringing about social and political upsets of a kind difficult to predict. This explains why the anxieties of Central Asian society centre not so much on theoretical arguments about the nature of the process of desiccation in the region, as on practical issues to do with how to make up the water deficit. The shortage of water in Central Asia is felt most keenly in agriculture, since in most of the region farming is impossible without irrigation. Land suitable for cultivation comprises about 25 million hectares, which exceeds the irrigation potential of the Central Asian rivers by 5 - 6 times[123], provoking the paradox that whilst there is land in abundance, there is no water to water it. It is true that the poor technical condition of the irrigation systems is responsible for very large losses of water; many experts placed no small hope on the reconstruction of the irrigation systems, in the belief that this would economize water both in order to save the Aral Sea and for agricultural purposes. However, subsequent calculations, made in the years 1989 - 90, showed that the reconstruction of the irrigation systems in the basin of the Aral Sea would save a mere 10 cubic kilometres of water per year, a saving which is utterly inadequate not merely for the salvation of the Aral Sea, but also in order to satisfy the fast-growing demands of the region's agricultural sector. Furthermore, reconstruction of this kind would cost a great deal (25 billion rubles - at 1989 prices) and require many years of work[124]. In the opinion of Philip Miklin, the American professor and well-known specialist on the water problems of the former USSR, a comprehensive modernization of the Central Asian irrigation systems would cost a lot more - as much as 100 billion rubles (at 1989 prices). Furthermore, Miklin is of the view that even if everything is done to economize in use of water, Central Asia's aquatic resources are nevertheless insufficient to cater for the future economic and social needs of the population - to say nothing of saving the Aral Sea[125]. The rapid increase in demand for water is a result not merely of the growing needs of industry and agriculture, but also of rapid growth amongst the Central Asian population. During the years of Soviet rule alone (1917 - 91), the population grew from 7 million to 50 million (including Russians), and continues to grow at a very rapid rate of almost 3% per year.

On the eve of the break-up of the USSR supporters of the salvation of the Aral Sea gave broad backing to the initiative of the Kazakh professor A. Tursunov, who proposed that water use should be compulsorily reduced by 20% and all reservoirs eliminated, their contents being emptied into the Aral Sea. Tursunov further proposed structural changes to the region's agricultural production, a substantial reduction in the proportion of water-intensive varieties amongst the cotton and rice crops, and development of cattle rearing, market gardening and vegetable production. This idea encountered a highly negative reaction amongst hydrologists, hydroelectricity specialists and economists alike, whose opinion was that elimination of reservoirs would mean the end of agriculture throughout the region, as well as entailing the disruption of the hydroelectric system. Irrigation-based farming would in that case survive only in the fluminal flood-lands, and there would be nothing with which to feed the population. This view gained extra strength from the fact that at the beginning of the 1990s the water level in all reservoirs was already below the red line and a large part of the cotton crop had perished for lack of water. The discharge of a further 20% of water into the Aral Sea would, according to these specialists, strike a terrible blow to the region's economy. A reduction in the cotton crop, on the other hand, might help to solve the problem of the deficit in food production, but would not save water, since, in spite of common opinion, the majority of agricultural crops require water in no smaller quantities than does cotton.

Unfortunately, water to save the Aral Sea is not to be found in Central Asia itself. Attempts to ward off ecological catastrophe in the Aral Sea region by rechannelling vitally scarce water into the Aral Sea will inevitably result in economic catastrophe in the region. However, the problem does not end there. By the beginning of the 21st century, even taking account of water saved as a result of allowing the Aral Sea to dry up, Central Asia will find itself facing a deficit of water resources. This will make the search for additional sources of water unavoidable. Desalination of sea water, as so widely practiced in countries such as Saudia Arabia, Kuwait and the Arab Emirates of the Persian Gulf, offers no solution to Central Asia's problems. Desalination is very expensive, on the one hand, and, on the other, Central Asia's water needs are very great indeed; consequently, what is feasible for coastal countries with small populations and large reserves of petrodollars, is absolutely beyond the reach of the densely populated, but poor states of Central Asia, which are, on top of everything else, far from the nearest supplies of sea water. The only remaining solution of the problem is to rechannel water from water-rich Siberia. As was stressed on the eve of the disintegration of the USSR by specialists on the problems of Central Asian water management, 'the Central Asian natural environment is already overloaded, which makes it necessary either to move the population out of the area, or to bring in water'[126].

The fact of a shortage of water in the Aral Sea and an excess of water in the Caspian Sea naturally suggested the idea of rechannelling water from one sea to the other. A project of this kind was put forward in 1993 by the Kazakh geographer Sch. Duisebaev. He proposed a Caspian-Aral canal over the Ustyurt plateau, and in this had the backing of many Central Asians including the Kazakhstan president Nursultan Nazarbaev, who is also head of the International Trust for the Salvation of the Aral Sea[127]. However, construction of such a canal would require sums of money which are beyond the pockets not merely of Kazakhstan, but of all the Central Asian states put together. The project's most serious defect, though, is that it does nothing to resolve the main problem in Central Asia - the shortage of fresh water. In view of the exceedingly high financial cost of the canal, this casts doubt on the value of the project.

The Project of Rechanneling Siberian Rivers into Central Asia

The largest and most expensive project in Soviet history was developed in the 1970s, then the Soviet leadership came up against the problem of the inability of water resources in Central Asia to feed an increase in cotton production. The original plan, work on which started as far back as 1969, contemplated redirecting part of the flow of rivers in Siberia (from the basin of the River Ob), directly into the Aral Sea, with a view to using water in the Central Asian rivers solely for agricultural purposes. However, as a result of the growing shortage of water in the main agricultural regions of Uzbekistan and Kazakhstan, and under pressure from the leadership of the latter republics, the government in Moscow was forced to make frequent revisions to the project's aims. In the last version of the project the course of the canal was to be almost 1000 km longer than in the original plan, and at least twice as expensive. Even more importantly, though, the final version discarded the initial goal of coming to the aid of the dying Aral Sea; water from Siberia would no longer make it to the sea. The history of the appearance of various versions of the project for redirecting water from Siberia is a supreme illustration of the threat of a rapid deterioration in the water balance in Central Asia: what had started out as a plan to improve the ecological situation in the Aral Sea region became an attempt to save the region's thirst-tortured economy. In the middle of the 1980s the project was approved by the Moscow administration , receiving the title of Sibaral (Siberia-Aral); work on its realization began. The exceedingly high cost of the project, however, and the risk of incurring ecological problems in those regions of Siberia whence it was planned to take water, the necessity of moving settlements from the path of the canal - all this provoked fierce resistance from both the leaderships of the Siberian regions and Russian society at large. The new Communist Party leadership which came to power in 1985 under Mikhail Gorbachev was more sensitive to public opinion, and for this reason took the decision to stop work on redirecting water from Siberia to Central Asia. Meanwhile, though, research related to the project was to continue. The new line adopted by the Moscow authorities was essentially that by the year 2010 Central Asia should be using only its own water resources and with all possible economy, and only subsequently was it planned to return to renewed consideration of the project. By the end of the 1980s, however, all research on the project had in fact come to a halt, and the break-up of the USSR made realization of the project unthinkable.

Water and Politics

If it has lost all relevance for Russia, however, this project continues to be of vital importance for the Central Asian states. Even if in future the Central Asian states succeed in carrying out the expensive reconstruction of the irrigation system and in organizing strict economy in water consumption, existing water resources will nevertheless be insufficient to cater for the needs of the rapidly-expanding population. The only radical solution of the water deficit in the region as whole - i.e. not merely in the area surrounding the Aral Sea - is to rechannel water from Siberia into Central Asia. By the first half of the 21st century the realization of such a project will be a matter of life and death for the majority of the Central Asian republics (with the possible exception of Kyrgyzstan and Tajikistan), and will play a decisive role in determining policy in these republics - if, that is, they have not already surrendered their independence from Russia. The water factor will emerge as having significantly more importance than Central Asian links with Turkey and Iran in the ethnic, cultural, linguistic and religious spheres. Water will become more valuable than Arabian petrodollars and more important than Western capital investment and technology. No single ideology - nationalism, Islamic fundamentalism, communism or liberalism - will be able to retain power in Central Asia if it does not supply the region with water. But water can come only from Russia, of which the Central Asian region was an inalienable part for more than 100 years. It cannot be doubted that both the present economic upheavals in Russia and the euphoria of independence amongst the Central Asian states will sooner or later pass, whilst the problem of the water shortage will not only remain, but will become even more acute. From the point of view of the near future Russia will have in its hands a unique lever of influence over the Central Asian republics, a means of applying pressure superior to all other means (e.g. Russian military garrisons, economic aid, the size of the local Russian minority population). It is no coincidence that the Central Asian republics were the only republics to resist the break-up of the USSR. And if a single centralized state similar to the USSR were to be restored, they would be the first to voluntarily join it. This stance is to be explained not by the dominance of the former communist leadership, but by factors of an economic nature. Of all the former Soviet republics, Central Asia was and remains the region most dependent on Russia. Until the break-up of the USSR, Moscow paid for between half and two thirds of the budgets of Central Asian republics, whilst the republics themselves were Russia's raw material-producing appendices, bound to her hand and foot. Uzbekistan, for example, was in effect given over in its entirety to the cotton monoculture. In contrast to former African and Asian colonies which have in time managed to overcome their absolute dependence on their colonial masters, the Central Asian states find themselves in a position which is aggravated by their fatal dependence on Russian water resources. The next few decades will reveal all the implications of this dependence, to which there is no alternative. It cannot be ruled out that Russia's future relations with the Central Asian states will echo the policy followed by Khiva in its relations with the Turkmen tribes of Mangyshlak, when the Khivan khans alternately released and shut off water over the now dried-up course of the Uzboi in order to secure the obedience of those restless tribes.

The deterioration of the water situation has already had repercussions on relations between the Central Asian republics, as is evidenced by the conflicts between Uzbekistan and Turkmenistan over use of water from the Amudarya. Water has become the main motive for confrontation between the Uzbeks and Kyrgyz in the Fergana Valley. It is worth noting that Turkic and Islamic solidarity recedes into the background when the issue at stake is division of such a precious resource as water. The forthcoming drafting of inter-state agreements regarding the distribution of water resources amongst the Central Asian states is sure to be the most difficult and troublesome problem that these states will have to face in their relations with each other.

Pollution of the Environment

The deficit of water in Central Asia has an aggravating effect on the region's second most important ecological problem - pollution of the environment. Even before the break-up of the USSR Central Asia boasted the highest level of pollution in the Soviet Union; declarations of independence have changed the situation only for the worse, since producers have become less controllable.

The greater part of the territory of Central Asia is occupied by desert, semi-desert and mountains. Life, and - to an even greater extent - agriculture are possible only where there is water, i.e. in river valleys, as a rule. This explains why the region's large population is concentrated in ten groups of oases which occupy relatively small areas of land. Population density in these oases is very high. In the Fergana Valley, for example, and particularly in its eastern part, density reaches 500 people per square kilometre, a figure which matches those for Holland and Japan. In Uzbekistan's Khorezm oblast the average population density is not much less - 200 people per square kilometre[128]. For this reason any kind of environmental pollution in these oases has an immediate and unpleasant effect on large numbers of people. A serious cause of pollution is the excessive use of chemical herbicides and pesticides on the cotton fields. In addition, the use of highly imperfect agricultural cotton-harvesting machinery makes necessary increased reliance on herbicides in order to eliminate green leaves that would otherwise impede the operation of the harvesters. As a result, use of chemical herbicides and pesticides in Central Asia stands at 20 - 25 kg per hectare, whereas the average for the former USSR as a whole is no more than 3 kg. The level of infection with viral hepatitis and other diseases caused by environmental pollution is 3 - 5 times higher than the Russian average[129]. As a result of the thoughtless use of fertilizer - many times exceeding amounts required - the earth on many cotton fields has become covered with a thin layer of salts and chemicals. Almost all women working in the fields suffer from a variety of illnesses caused by pollution of the environment. Everywhere there is an insufficiency of drinking water. For example, in the Vahsh Valley of Tadjikistan, an area with a population of one million at the present time, little more than 30% of inhabitants have tap-water; in the main, people drink polluted water from irrigation ditches fed with water running off the cotton fields.[130]

A large part of the blame for environmental pollution in the region is to be borne by the chemical industry, which is the second largest sector of the economy after the cotton agro-industrial complex. The negative effects of the region's chemical producers are considerably magnified by specific geographical and climatic factors responsible for Central Asia's high population density, as well as by the shortage of water. The intensive development of the chemical industry under Soviet rule was a result of the communist leadership's desire to provide work for as many as possible of the local unskilled labour force. Until the middle of the 1970s problems of environmental pollution in former Soviet Central Asia were not taken seriously, since the guiding policy was the fastest possible economic and social development of the region. As a result, most manufacturing plant is either not fitted with pollution-reduction equipment at all or is fitted with equipment in poor working condition. An investigation into the rivers of Uzbekistan, conducted in the summer of 1989, found ecological and sanitary/epidemiological conditions in the basins of almost all rivers to be extremely critical. Pollution through chemical waste products and chemical fertilizers is far in excess of all tolerable norms. Similarly alarming is the quantity of harmful organic substances in the water. Nevertheless it should be pointed out that the main cause of atmospheric pollution (responsible for 60 - 70% of pollution) is not the chemical industry, but automobile transport, the greater part of which is in poor mechanical condition[131].

Amongst sources of environmental pollution in Central Asia, radioactive contamination occupies a special place. This however is localized in character. Radioactivity has accumulated over many years in eastern Kazakhstan, in the region of the city of Semipalatinsk, the site of systematic nuclear weapons tests. Ground-level and atmospheric tests with atomic and hydrogen warheads continued right up to the signing of the agreement banning surface nuclear explosions; frequently, as happened in the 1950s, such tests were conducted without even elementary precautionary measures. As a result, land and water sources throughout the vast territory of eastern Kazakhstan have been affected by serious radioactive contamination, which has a tendency to spread towards Kazakhstan's densely populated industrial and agricultural regions. Although nuclear testing has now ceased entirely, background radiation remains at an alarming level. Furthermore, the regions of eastern Kazakhstan are periodically subject to the danger of radioactive contamination from atomic weapons tests carried out in the neighbouring Chinese province of Xingjiang.

Soil Erosion

This problem mainly concerns Kazakhstan, where it was provoked by changes in Soviet economic policy in the second half of the 1950s. In an attempt to cover the deficit in food production (and especially in grain) central Communist Party organs, at the initiative of Nikita Kruschev, put their approval to a scheme of grandiose proportions - to plough up and put into agricultural use tens of millions of hectares of virgin land in Kazakhstan. It has to be pointed out that both before and after the imposition of Soviet rule in Central Asia, the most eminent Russian, and subsequently Soviet, specialists argued against the ploughing up of these lands, taking the view that a project of this kind would be either pointless or actually dangerous in its possible consequences. The greater part of land due to be ploughed up was in the zone of so-called 'risk cultivation', an area suffering from periodic droughts and strong winds and possessing a layer of fertile soil that was excessively thin and vulnerable. It seems that in ancient times farmers knew the dangers associated with this land, for in the past it was never cultivated, but merely used as good pasture-land for cattle. In the Middle Ages this part of to-day's Kazakhstan was known as Desht-i Kypchak; here tribes of Kypchaks (Polovtsians) led a nomad life, driving huge herds of cattle from one pasture to another.

Wholesale and frequently incorrect ploughing up of this pasture-land confirmed the fears of the scientists. The thin layer of fertile soil, which had earlier been held in place by grass and the latter's powerful root system, soon began to blow away in the wind. Serious soil erosion set in; the strong winds characteristic of the area turned into dust storms. After the first years of relatively good harvests came droughts and a sharp decline in soil fertility. Doubt was thrown upon the economic value of cultivating the virgin lands. The average annual size of grain harvests began to fall at a steady rate; in the 1980s, for example, harvests were smaller than in the 1970s[132]. The massive-scale ploughing up of the virgin lands caused considerable loss to cattle-rearing in the area, as cattle were deprived of their former pasture-land. At the same time, the additional grain yield from Kazakhstan turned out to be smaller and more expensive than anticipated, whilst the main effect of this improperly thought-through piece of human economic action was the appearance of a new ecological problem in Central Asia - large-scale soil erosion in Kazakhstan.

Seismic Activity

The existing serious ecological dangers in Central Asia are aggravated by a problem that has affected the region from the earliest times - its liability to destructive earthquakes. Seismographers consider Central Asia to be one of the worst regions for seismic activity in the former USSR, a situation which is made worse still by the fact that almost all the Central Asian oases with a high population density are in seismically active regions. This fact finds confirmation in architectural monuments surviving from the time of Timur, the majority of which have been ruined not so much by wars or time, as by powerful earthquakes. The most devastating and well-known earthquakes in recent times were in Ashkhabad, the capital of Turkmenistan, in 1946, and in Tashkent, the capital of Uzbekistan, in 1966. In the first case a powerful earthquake practically wiped the entire city together with its inhabitants from the face of the earth; in the second, a large part of Tashkent suffered devastation and tens of thousands of people perished or were wounded. Several major, but less powerful earthquakes have occurred in Kyrgyzstan and Tadjikistan. Hardly a year goes by without news coming in from these republics of subterranean tremors of various strengths. Earthquakes in these areas have become a natural calamity of an everyday kind. However, the intensive construction at the beginning of the 1960s of dams and hydro-electric stations in the mountain areas of Tadjikistan and Kyrgyzstan has given rise to a new ecological problem - the threat of flooding in densely populated areas in the event of damage caused to these dams following an earthquake. Moreover, the very fact that dams have been built in high mountain areas prone to seismic activity, and the storing of large volumes of water under pressure, could lead to rock falls, displacements of earth and so to the destruction of the dams. A typical example from this point of view is the Nurek dam, built in a seismically active part of the mountains of Tadjikistan in the 1970s and 1980s. In spite of the fact that account was taken of the likelihood of earthquakes when building the dam, the possibility of its destruction in the event of a particularly large subterranean tremor is something that no specialist can fully rule out entirely. Rising concern over the danger of ecological catastrophe of this kind resulted, in the middle of the 1980s, in the freezing of all similar construction projects in Kyrgyzstan. In recent years tectonic changes in the basin of the Aral Sea have produced a deterioration of seismic conditions in many regions of Central Asia. Due to a rise in the subterranean water-level, a number of major Central Asian cities located near large underground basins are today less secure from the threat of seismic activity than 20 years ago[133].

Conclusion

The present critical ecological situation in Central Asia is the product of several factors: the shortage of water, environmental pollution, soil erosion, and the construction of dams at high altitudes in regions susceptible to earthquakes. All these factors are the result of human activity. Natural factors, such as the general tendency towards desiccation in Central Asia or seismic activity, play a secondary role - being, as far as we can tell, of a cyclical character and merely aggravating the results of Man's thoughtless economic interventions. The main ecological problem in Central Asia is the shortage of water caused both by the high natural growth rate of the population and by careless use of water resources. The drying-up of the Aral Sea is only one part of a problem which is universal throughout Central Asia, although it is perhaps the most dramatic and impressive example of this problem. The Central Asian water deficit can be solved - and the Aral Sea saved from desiccation - only by redirecting water from Siberia into Central Asia. The break-up of the USSR has made execution of such a scheme more difficult, although it does not rule out the project's being returned to at some date in the future. There can be no doubt that in the next few decades the water factor will come to play a critical role in the region's economic and political decision making alike, a situation which is objectively in the interests of Russia. The need for a water-saving policy will inevitably force large changes in the structure of Central Asia's agriculture and industry. In the foreseeable future, the water deficit will necessitate a reduction in plantings of cotton and rice, and the reorientation of industry towards sectors which consume least water and cause least harm to the environment (research-intensive industry, for example). However, the present lack of an alternative source of hard currency to replace cotton and the need to increase food production to meet the demands of a fast-growing population make real changes to the present structure of agriculture impossible. The high level of unemployment, on the one hand, and, on the other, the lack of a highly-qualified workforce make it unrealistic to expect rapid changes in the structure of industry. Modern research-intensive industry calls for a small but well-qualified workforce and, most importantly of all, for large capital investment, of which there is a lack in Central Asia. The economization of water resources, the reconstruction of agricultural irrigation systems and the equipment of industry with pollution-reduction devices will also require large sums of money, which the Central Asian states do not possess. As a result, the situation with water in Central Asia will steadily deteriorate, and this will have an increasing effect on the political orientation of the Central Asian republics, as well as on their relations with each other. At the same time, though, the degree to which different states in Central Asia suffer from ecological problems varies considerably. For example, although the shortage of fresh water is universal throughout Central Asia, worst-off for water resources are Uzbekistan, Turkmenistan and Kazakhstan, whilst Kyrgyzstan and Tadjikistan are comparatively well-supplied with water. Environmental pollution follows a similar pattern. Uzbekistan and Kazakhstan, being the republics with the largest populations and the most advanced agriculture and industry, are the worst polluted.

Truly serious discussion of ecological problems in the USSR began only in the second half of the 1980s during Gorbachev's period of 'perestroika' and 'glasnost'. Pressure of public opinion, a factor which local and central government in the USSR found itself facing for the first time, led to the cancellation of many ecologically dangerous projects, including in Central Asia. The subsequent break-up of the USSR considerably complicated the ecological situation in Central Asia, since the states of the region were in no condition to resolve their ecological problems on their own. The break-up had highly negative consequences for the fate of a project of the utmost importance for the region - the rechannelling of water from Siberia into Central Asia. In the foreseeable future, however, the progressive water deficit will force Central Asia into dependence on Russian water; this will be reflected in changes in economic and political direction amongst the Central Asian states.

Epilogue

It has been twenty years since the break-up of the Soviet Union. Yet the political regimes in all five Central Asian states have not changed: power remains aggregated in the hands of ex-communist leaders, who do not tolerate any opposition. Only two countries, Kyrgyzstan and Turkmenistan, underwent leadership replacement; these changes, however, did not bring about any significant modifications in their political regimes. The positive feature of these authoritarian regimes is their unquestionable secularism and ability to maintain a decent degree of stability within their states. However, the cost associated with such stability and secularism is the antidemocratic and repressive behavior of the authorities.

In foreign politics, all of the Central Asian countries attempt to balance their relations with Russia and United States, although some of them, like Uzbekistan, favor the U.S., while others, such as Kyrgyzstan, tilt toward Russia. The influence of other players in the Central Asian political arena – that of China, Turkey, Iran and the European Union – is limited to economy and financial matters. The special status of Turkey's relations with the four Turkic-speaking states, which existed in the 1990s, has virtually disappeared as of today. Erdogan's government bears sole responsibility for this. The new course towards the Islamization of Turkey and rejection of Kemalists' pro-Western orientation alarmed the secular regimes of Central Asia, and made the Turkish model of development unacceptable for them. However, neighboring Iran also failed in its efforts to strengthen its influence in the region. As the last two decades have shown, the aggressive and fanatical Islamic regime in Iran has taken aback, without exception, all of the Central Asian states, including Farsi-speaking Tajikistan. Only the Turkic-speaking Turkmenistan, the weakest country in the region militarily, and furthermore, the only one having an extended border with Iran, is obliged, more than any other of the states in Central Asia, to abide by the temperament in Teheran.

The American 2001 wartime movements in Afghanistan attracted attention to the Central Asian states and classified them as potential allies in the battle against the Taliban, while the growth of anti-Western sentiments in Pakistan made the American supply bases in Central Asia, particularly in Manas (Kyrgyzstan), irreplaceable. The planned 2014 departure of NATO's armed forces from Afghanistan enlarges, in the short term, the role of Central Asian states for the West, while on the other hand, threatens them with long-term uncertainty, and possibly, a new obliviousness in the future.

The exodus of Russian and Russian-speaking populations from Central Asia continued unremittingly throughout the twenty years after the collapse of the Soviet Union. In 1992, almost 11 million Russians lived there, while as of 2012, their number has decreased twofold. Today, the majority of the Russian population remains only within Kazakhstan and Kyrgyzstan, where it continues to play a significant role in the economy, politics, and culture of these countries. A Russian minority still lives in Uzbekistan, particularly in the capital, Tashkent, but its influence there is inconsequential. As for the other two Central Asian states, Tajikistan and Turkmenistan, there are practically no Russians there – almost all of them have emigrated. The civil war in Tajikistan (1992-93) and the 'Turkmenization' policies of President Niyazov and that of his successor, Gurbanguli Berdimuhamedov, resulted in massive emigration of the Russian population there. The abrupt diminution of the Russian and Russian-speaking populations potentially decreases Russia's influence in this region while stabilizing national sovereignty of the Central Asian states.

During their twenty years of independence, three Central Asian states – Turkmenistan, Uzbekistan and Kazakhstan – acquired a new source of income through the export of oil and gas. According to geological estimates, Central Asia possesses large supplies of these energy resources particularly that of gas, which could, in perspective, significantly improve the economic positions of the countries of that region and ease off the supply pressures in the world market of oil and gas. However, the oil and gas production is restricted by the absence of oil and gas pipelines, not allowing the connection of Central Asia with consumers in Europe and Asia. Motivated to receive control over the transportation of the strategically important raw materials, Russia insists on laying oil and gas pipelines solely across her own territory. Attempting to avert the building of a gas pipeline on the bottom of the Caspian Sea, Russia even hinted at the possibility of using military force 'in case of any violation of the Caspian Sea's particular status.' Therefore, Turkmenistan, unprepared to confront Russia, but also disliking the prospect of obeying her dictate, found a different solution – supplying China with its gas.

Unfortunately, throughout their years of independence, the Central Asian states have not managed to resolve a single ecological problem of their region; even worse – they allowed the issues to grow unimpeded. Saving the Aral Sea failed; it dried, leaving only a few small, shallow lakes. The water deficit in Central Asia continues to escalate due to populations' growth and the continued development of industry and agriculture. As the situation worsens with the onset of each year, water is becoming an area of continuous conflict between peoples and even states. Because of the conflicts regarding the distribution of water supply, bloody confrontations occur between the Uzbeks, Kyrgyz, and Tajiks in the fertile Fergana Valley. For example, the construction of the Rogun Dam instigated a serious conflict between Tajikistan and Uzbekistan. Tajikistan is in need of water and electrical energy, which the powerful Rogun Dam can freely give. Neighboring Uzbekistan, however, fears that the construction of the 335-meter-high dam in a seismically dangerous location will threaten the Uzbek territory and population with a possible, disastrous ecological catastrophe. Russia, without the aid of which the construction of this dam would have been impossible, views it as a 'carrot' for its ally, Tajikistan, and as a 'stick' for the disobedient Uzbekistan.

Overall, the time after the break-up of the Soviet Union has shown that the ruling elite of all of the Central Asian states made a unilateral choice in favor of the authoritarian, secular regime, free market, and the attraction of foreign investments on a large scale. The only real threat to this choice is posed not by weak democratic oppositions but by the radical Islamist groups, the activities of which are considered illegal. As witnessed by the events in Tunis and Egypt in 2011, authoritarian secular regimes can be very vulnerable if Islamists effectively use economic difficulties and social tension. In order to avoid the capture of power by Islamist fundamentalists, the currently governing elites in Central Asia not only need to depend on their repressive apparatuses in battle with their opponents, but also attempt to effectively resolve the accumulated economic and social problems of their respective nations.

Bibliography

[1] Pravda Vostoka, Tashkent, 4.01.89, p.2.

[2] The Communist Party of the Soviet Union.

[3] F. Burlatskiy, Posle Stalina, *Novy Mir*, Moscow, 1988, No. 10, p.196.

[4] Izvestiya, 12.02.92.

[5] Izvestiya, 5.02.92; also, ITAR-TASS, 14.01.95.

[6] Kazakhstanskaya pravda, 30.04.92; also, Vestnik Kazakhstana, 11.06.94.

[7] Kazakhstanskaya pravda, 14.03.92; also, Sovety Kazakhstana, 20.06.94.

[8] Izvestiya, 14.02.92.

[9] Izvestiya, 8.01.92.

[10] The All-Union Communist Party of Bolsheviks.

[11] A. Akramov, *Bratskaya pomosch russkogo naroda v stroitelstve sotsializma v Uzbekistane*, Tashkent, 1982, p.71.

[12] Leninskiy sbornik, vol.34, p. 326.

[13] *Istoriya Uzbekskoy SSR*, vol.II, Tashkent, 1957, p.225.

[14] 'Na istoricheskom rubezhe.' *Sbornik o natsionalno-gosudarstven-nom razmezhevanii Sredney Azii*, Tashkent, 1924, p.22.

[15] E. Zelkina, *Ocherki po agrarnomu voprosu v Sredney Azii*, Moscow, 1930, p.8.

[16] Kh. Salimov, *Naselenie Sredney Azii*, Tashkent, 1975, p.97.

[17] Kommunist Tadjikistana, Dushanbe, 21.07.89, p.1.

[18] Russian Soviet Federative Socialist Republic.

[19] Bakinskiy rabochiy, Baku, 5.05.92.

[20] Nezavisimaya gazeta, 15.05.1992.

[21] Ibid.

[22] B.A. Litvinskiy, Istoricheskie sudby Vostochnogo Turkestana i Sredney Azii (problemy etnokulturnoy obschnosti). Sb: *Vostochniy Turkestan i Srednaya Aziya*, Moscow, 1984, p.4.

[23] Ibid, p.14..

[24] N.E. Bekmakhanova, *Mnogonatsionalnoe naselenie Kazakhstana i Kyrgyzii v epokhu capitalisma*, Moscow, 1986, p.171.

[25] Ibid, p.160.

[26] Ibid, p.174.

[27] *Istoriya uzbekskogo naroda*, Tashkent, 1952, p.287.

[28] *Istoriya Uzbekskoy SSR*, v.2, Tashkent, 1957, p.243.

[29] N.A. Voznesenskiy, *Voennaya ekonomika SSSR v period Otechestvennoy voiny*, Moscow, 1948, p.41.

[30] *Istoricheskiy opyt stroitelstva sotsialisma v respublikakh Sredney Asii*, Moscow, 1968, p.124.

[31] *Naseleniye Sredney Asii*, Moscow, 1985, p.16.

[32] H. Salimov, *Naseleniye Sredney Asii*, Tashkent, 1975, p.91.

[33] M. Rywkin, *Russia in Central Asia*, London, 1963, p.86.

[34] Kazakhstanskaya pravda, 13.07.89.

[35] Komsomolskaya pravda, 9.02.94.

[36] Ibid.

[37] Kommunist Tajikistana, 7.07.89.

[38] Literaturnaya gazeta, 26.07.89, p.10.

[39] Yegor Ligachev, Gdlyan i drugiye .... , chapter from '*Zagadka Gorbacheva*', Moscow, 1991, p.27.

[40] Pravda Vostoka, 15.07.90.

[41] Moskovskiye novosty, 13.12.92.

[42] Sovety Kazakhstana, 11.09.93.

[43] Izvestiya, 12.02.94, p.3.

[44] ITIM, 3.02.93.

45 Ibid.

46 *Istoriya tadzhikskogo naroda, vol. II*, Moscow, 1964, p.184.

47 *Istoriya Uzbekskoy SSR*, Tashkent, 1957, p.203.

48 *Etnicheskie protsessy u natsionalnykh grupp Sredney Azii i Kazakhstana*, Moscow, Nauka, 1980, p.203.

49 *Istoriya Uzbekskoy SSR*, Tashkent, 1957, p.314.

50 *Vsesoyuznye perepisi naseleniya*, 1959, 1970, 1989.

51 D.I. Logofet, *Strana bespraviya*, St Petersburg, 1909, p.59.

52 E. Zelkina, *Ocherki po agrarnomu voprosu v Sredney Azii*, Moscow,1930, pp. 35 - 36.

53 *Istoriya Uzbekskoy SSR*, Tashkent, 1957, p.285.

54 *KPSS v rezolyutsiyakh i rescheniyakh syezdov, konferentsiy, plenumov TsK*, vol.4, Moscow,1970, p.323.

55 M. Rywkin, *Russia in Central Asia*, New York, 1963, p.91.

56 *Courier UNESCO*, 1981, September-October, p.29.

57 A. Akhmedov, *Islam v sovremennoy ideyno-politicheskoy borbe*, Moscow, 1985, p.143.

58 Ibid, p.129.

59 *Religion and Atheism in the USSR and Eastern Europe*, London, 1975, p.99.

60 H. Carrere d'Encausse, *L'empire eclate*, Paris, 1978, p.278.

61 ITAR-TASS, 26.03.92.

62 Ibid, 21.01.1992.

63 Ibid, 25.12.1992.

64 Ibid, 10.01.1993.

65 Ibid.

66 *S. Peterburgskie vedomosti*, 16.02.1994, p.4.

67 Ibid.

68 ITAR-TASS, 15.07.1992.

69 Ibid, 10.04.1993.

70 *Istoriya Uzbekskoy SSR*, vol II, Tashkent, 1957, p.115.

[71] Y. Zelkina, *Ocherki po agrarnomu voprosu v Sredney Azii*, Moscow, 1930, p.27.

[72] Masalskiy, *Khlopkovodstvo v Sredney Azii*, St Petersburg, 1892.

[73] M.Mamedov, *Irrigatsiya Sredney Azii*, Moscow, 1969, pp.16-17.

[74] Demidov, *Ekonomicheskie ocherki khlopkovodstva, khlopkovoy torgovli i promyschlennosti v Turkestane*, St Petersburg, 1910, p.42.

[75] Fedorov, *Khlopkovodstvo Sredney Azii*, Moscow, 1898, p.100.

[76] 'Melkiy selskiy kredit', *Materiali senatskoy komissii Palena*, 1911.

[77] *Byulleten khlopkovogo komiteta*, No.3, 1913.

[78] '*Materiali senatskoy revizii*', pt. 1. section 2, p.532.

[79] '*Voprosi kolonizatsii*', No.21, 1912, pp.311-316.

[80] Demidov, op. cit, p.65.

[81] *Istoricheskiy opyt stroitelstva sotsializma v respublikakh Sredney Azii*, Moscow, 1968, p.105.

[82] *Ekonomika promyshlennosti respublik Sredney Azii*, Tashkent, 1983, p.161.

[83] Pravda Vostoka, 13.01.90, p.2.

[84] L.A. Alibekov, *Schedrost pustyni*, Moscow, 1988, p.54.

[85] Argumenty i fakti, 26.08.89; Kazakhstanskaya pravda, 6.07.89.

[86] Kommunist Tadjikistana, 1.07.89, p.2.

[87] Kommunist Tadjikistana, 7.07.89, p.3.

[88] Ibid.

[89] M.A. Olimov, Etalon nekapitalisticheskogo razvitiya? - *Narodyi Azii i Afriki*, Moscow, 1989, No. 4, p.22.

[90] Pravda Vostoka, 26.01.89, p.2; 24.01.89, p.1.

[91] Ibid, 20.01.89.

[92] Pravda Vostoka, 3.03.90.

[93] Ibid; also, Pravda Vostoka, 16.07.89.

[94] Yegor Ligachev, Gdlyan i drugie .... (chapter from the book '*Zagadka Gorbacheva*', Moscow, 1991, p.16).

[95] Ibid, p.27.

[96] *Sredneaziatskiy ekonomicheskiy raion*, Moscow, 1972, p.145.

[97] Ibid, p.176.

[98] Pravda Vostoka, 4.01.90.

[99] *Ekonomika i zhizn*, Moscow, 1993, No.6, p.19.

[100] Izvestiya, 24.05.93.

[101] Kazakhstanskaya pravda, 6.07.1989.

[102] Argumenty i fakty, 26.08.1989

[103] Pravda vostoka, 01.07.1989, p.3.

[104] Ibid.

[105] Pravda vostoka, 7.03.1989, p.2.

[106] Ibid, 28.03.1990.

[107] Rossiyskaya gazeta, 15.02.1994, p.6.

[108] Moskovskie Novosti, No. 26, 1994.

[109] Arrian, *Pokhod Alexandra*, Moscow, 1993, p.138.

[110] L.N. Gumilyev, *Drevnaya Rus i Velikaya Step (Ot Rusi do Rossii)*, St Petersburg, 1992, p.83.

[111] L.A. Vayner, *Ivan Vasilyevich Muschketov i ego rol v poznanii geologii Sredney Azii*, Tashkent, 1954.

[112] V. A. Obruchev, *Izbraniye raboty po geografii Azii*, vol.1, Moscow, 1951.

[113] I.A. Rezanov, *Po goram i pustynyam Azii: Puteschestviya K.I. Bgdanovicha*, Moscow, 1976.

[114] V.V. Bartold, *Sochineniya*, vol.2 and 3, Moscow, 1963.

[115] L.S. Berg, *Izbranniye trudy*, vol.3, Moscow, 1960.

[116] A.I. Voeikov, *Vozdeystvie cheloveka na prirodu*, Moscow, 1963.

[117] K.K. Markov, *Pyat let po Pamiru (itogi pamirskikh ekspeditsiy 1928, 1929, 1931, 1932, 1933 gg)*, Moscow-Leningrad, 1935.

[118] E.M. Murzaev, *V dalekoy Azii, ocherki po istorii izucheniya Sredney i Tsentralnoy Azii v XIV - XX vekakh*, Moscow, 1956.

[119] A.G. Babaev, *Pustinya Kara-Kumi*, Ashkhabad, 1963.

[120] A.A. Alibekov, *Schedrost pustyni*, Moscow, 1988, p.51.

[121] Ibid, p.54.

[122] Ibid, p.41.

[123] *Sredneaziatskiy ekonomicheskiy rayon*, Moscow, 1972, p.145.

[124] Pravda Vostoka, 28.03.1990.

[125] Ibid.

[126] Sovety Kazakhstana, 2.09.1993.

[127] ITAR-TASS, 10.02.1994.

[128] Alibekov, op. cit, p.79.

[129] Kommunist Tadjikistana, 7.07.1989.

[130] Ibid, 1.07.1989, p.2.

[131] Pravda Vostoka, 5.01.1990.

[132] Kazakhstanskaya pravda, 25.07.1989, p.2..

[133] Pravda Vostoka, 13.03.1990.

Index